Reading Comprehension Education in Fifteen Countries

An Empirical Study

Robert L. Thorndike

With a Foreword by Torsten Husén

A Halsted Press Book
John Wiley & Sons
New York – London – Sydney – Toronto

Almqvist & Wiksell
Stockholm

Library of Congress Catalog Card Number 73-8049
Halsted Press ISBN 0-470-86235-1
Almqvist & Wiksell ISBN 91-20-03887-9

Design Dick Hallström

Printed in Sweden by
Almqvist & Wiksell Informationsindustri AB
Uppsala 1973

428.4
T499r

14-2263

INTERNATIONAL ASSOCIATION FOR THE EVALUATION
OF EDUCATIONAL ACHIEVEMENT (IEA)

International Studies
in Evaluation III

Contents

Foreword

It is a privilege for me to introduce the present report on the IEA International Study of Reading Comprehension. Like the studies conducted by IEA in other subject areas, this one has also been in many respects a pioneering venture.

The feasibility study conducted by IEA in 1959–1961 comprised *inter alia* a set of Reading Comprehension items (Foshay, 1962). Professor Robert L. Thorndike of Teachers College, Columbia University, who conducted the data processing and statistical analysis of that project, found that, contrary to expectations, the international variance in relation to the intranational one was smaller for reading items than for other test material. Furthermore, there was a remarkable consistency across nations in the item statistics. Thus it did seem possible, in spite of the formidable translation problems, to administer verbal tests internationally. The language barrier could be broken. As a result, Professor Thorndike and his students later pursued studies pertaining to the adequate translation of reading passages from one language to another.

Therefore, when the IEA Council decided in 1966 to launch an international study of Reading Comprehension as part of its Six Subject Survey, we were happy to have Professor Thorndike accept to serve as Chairman of the International Reading Comprehension Committee which was set up to develop the rationale and the instruments for the cross-national study.

The present report on this international investigation of Reading Comprehension shows that it is in fact possible to measure reading achievement in a reliable way and to make meaningful cross-national comparisons. A single test of reading speed was also developed which has been of particular value in evaluating reading competency in children from less developed countries, where the overwhelming majority of students come from illiterate homes and have to be taught reading under very disadvantaged conditions in comparison with their age-mates in the richer countries. Even though great care was taken in the selection of the reading passages to be included in the tests to make sure that their content was as universal as possible, and in spite of all efforts to translate the passages as accurately as possible, translation problems could not be avoided entirely. These problems were particularly troublesome in connection with the development of a test of word knowledge.

Achievements in Reading Comprehension, like those in, for instance, Mathematics or Science, seem to lend themselves readily to international comparisons. They can be used as criteria in attempts to explore multinationally how various input factors of home background and school resources account for student and school differences. As in the Science and Literature studies (see Comber and Keeves, 1973, and Purves, 1973), these differences have been studied by means of stepwise multiple regression analyses. The replicative nature of such analyses has hopefully added to the generalizability of the findings. Certain pervading problems, such as the effect of school structure and age of school entry, as well as sex differences, have also been studied.

Particular thanks are due to those who carried the direct responsibility for designing the present study and who were responsible for the data processing, the statistical analyses, the writing up and the editing of the present report.

On behalf of IEA I should like in the first place to express our gratitude to Professor Thorndike, who not only served as Chairman of the International Reading Comprehension Committee, but also took on the burdensome task of writing the present volume. Furthermore, as a member of the IEA Technical Committee, Professor Thorndike played an important role in planning the statistical analyses related to the present as well as to other subject areas covered by the IEA surveys. Our thanks are also due to the other members of the International Committee, Dr Lily Ayman (Iran), Mme Françoise Bacher (France), Mr Alan C. Brimer (England), and Dr Jan Vastenhouw (The Netherlands).

Obviously, the tasks of coordination as well as of data processing in a project such as this have been enormous. Thanks are due first of all to Dr T. Neville Postlethwaite, who served as Executive Director of the project until the major analyses of the Stage 2 data were completed. The data processing units in New York and Stockholm had to deal with many unexpected complexities and had too to work under the pressures of a tight timetable. I should like to thank Messrs Mats Carlid, and John K. Hall, and Dr Richard M. Wolf for the assistance they have rendered IEA. We are also indebted to all those at IEA International in Stockholm who contributed in many ways to the reporting during the analyses, writing up and editing.

We are also deeply indebted to those who financially and in other respects sponsored this multi-funded project. IEA has adhered to the principle that costs incurred in connection with the work at the national level should be covered by funds raised within the respective countries, whereas international costs, such as keeping international headquarters and conducting data processing across countries, should be defrayed from funds raised by IEA as an organization. We would like to express our gratitude to the Bank of Sweden Tercentenary Fund, the Ford Foundation, the Leverhulme Trust, the Stiftung Volkswagenwerk, and the United States Office of Education, who together contributed the considerable funds needed for this venture. We are also indebted to UNESCO, under whose auspices this international research was initiated. IEA must also thank the Swedish Government for support both direct and indirect and the Chancellor of the Swedish Universities for his generous grant towards data processing costs. The printing of the present volume has been supported by a grant from the Bank of Sweden Tercentenary Fund.

The present survey of Reading Comprehension in 15 countries of enormous sociocultural diversity has considerably extended our knowledge basis with regard to evaluation of reading ability. It will hopefully also constitute a basis for studies in depth of factors influencing the acquisition of basic reading skills, an area in which IEA has already conducted some exploratory work.

Stockholm, Institute for the Study of
International Problems in Education, 1973

Torsten Husén
Chairman of IEA

11

Chapter 1

Introduction

There would be little argument that reading has been and probably will continue to be a central part of the school curriculum, especially the curriculum in the elementary grades. Literacy is the foundation on which the great bulk of education has proceeded, and its importance in the educational scene is attested to not only by the attention that is paid to it within the classroom but also by the enormous literature that has developed around the teaching of reading and the process of learning to read. This being the case, it seemed eminently appropriate that in a program devoted to empirical comparative education, comparative studies of progress in reading should be included.

In many ways, the most interesting cross-national comparisons having to do with learning to read would be comparisons of progress made during the first years of the elementary school. This is the level at which the basic decoding processes are established, and in which the equivalence between oral language and the written symbolism is mastered by the learner. In many ways, comparisons from country to country and from language to language of this initial decoding progress represent the most intriguing of the possible cross-national studies. However, empirical cross-national studies with seven- or eight-year-old children present particular difficulties. The skills of attending to and following directions so as to be testable in a group setting are poorly established at these ages, and the mechanics of data collection promised to be unduly burdensome if testing were to be carried out on an individual basis. Furthermore, within the context of the larger enterprise of which this particular study is a part, it was necessary to fit the testing of reading into the same framework that was used for testing Science, Literature, Civic Education, and English and French as Foreign Languages. In these other subject areas, much of the interest centered on the final yield of mastery at the end of the years of public education. Consequently, much of the emphasis was focussed on testing at age 14, an age that approximated the end of compulsory schooling, and at the final year of secondary education. There was some interest in testing at the end of the period of elementary education, defined as the period during which a child spent most of the day in a single classroom taught by a single teacher, and so it was agreed that some testing should be done of 10-year-old children. However, in none of the other academic fields in which testing was to be undertaken were the investigators interested in children below the age of 10, so it was not possible to test beginning reading in the context of the present study.

As indicated above, the testing of reading was fitted into a larger total program in which testing was being carried out in five other subject areas, and three main levels for data collection were included, to wit: 10-year-olds, 14-year-olds, and those in the final year of secondary education. (In some countries, limited data were gathered for an intermediate sample between the 14-year-olds and those in the final year of secondary education, but this group receives no attention in the report that follows.)

In some ways, the development of appropriate assessment materials in reading was easier than it was in the other subject areas that were involved in the IEA studies; in some ways, the development was harder. In the field of reading, there seems to be much more consensus as to the objectives of instruction. Each country would accept without question, we believe, the proposition that it is desirable that children learn to read with complete comprehension materials of a variety of styles and contents and to read them at a relatively rapid rate. The particular emphasis on different types of reading material—expository as opposed to literary, prose as opposed to poetry, etc.—might vary to some extent from country to country and also from school to school within a country, but there would be general agreement that children should be able to get meaning efficiently from written material of various styles and content areas.

On the other hand, the preparation of genuinely equivalent tests in reading, where the essence of the task involves very intimately the language of a particular country, would seem to present very serious difficulties. It seems axiomatic that the only possible way that the comparability of reading tests from one language to another can be established is through the use of common texts and common sets of questions upon them. However, the common texts must necessarily be translated into all of the languages in which the testing is to be done and perhaps, more seriously, the questions and response options to the questions (assuming that one is using a multiple-choice type of test) must also be translated. Very serious questions can be raised as to the comparability in difficulty of a passage and a set of questions on it when these have undergone translation.

There is some evidence that the difficulties related to translation are not as severe as one might anticipate. In the first of the present series of studies (Foshay, 1962) a short reading test was included, and it was found at that time that the difficulty of the test was rather uniform from country to country. The reading test showed less variation from country to country than either an arithmetic test or a non-verbal intelligence test. Furthermore, even the relative difficulty of the specific passages and specific items was highly stable from country to country and language to language. Within languages, the typical cross-country correlation of item difficulties was in the high 90's and even across languages the typical correlation in this pilot study was about 0.90. Subsequently, Kumbaraci (1966) studied the translation of material at a higher difficulty level from English into Turkish and back into English again. The test materials were those suitable for individuals entering college. With this more advanced and somewhat more select group, the correlation of item difficulties across languages was lower, being only about 0.70. However, it was found in this case that a back translation of the test that had been translated from English into Turkish yielded a new test in English that had very nearly the same properties as the original. It appeared in this instance that the test did not suffer much distortion through a double sequence of translation from English into Turkish and back from Turkish into English.

Encouraged by these two studies, the IEA Council agreed to include reading as one of the subject matter areas to be studied in its major project in cross-national testing. It was recognized that problems would undoubtedly arise in maintaining comparability of the reading material across translation but it was felt that with some care the test could be maintained as nearly enough the same task from one language to another to make the cross-national comparisons interesting and fruitful.

As in each of the subject areas in which IEA has carried out surveys, the administrative pattern was to bring together an International Committee to be directly responsible for preparation of the reading tests, for specifying the background data to be gathered about examinees, and for setting forth hypotheses to be investigated. The working membership of this Committee consisted of

Dr Lily Ayman, Teachers College, Tehran, Iran

Mme Françoise Bacher, Institut National d'Etude du Travail et d'Orientation Professionnelle, Paris, France

Mr Alan C. Brimer, Director, Educational Research Institute, Institute of Education, University of Bristol, England

Dr Jan Vastenhouw, Institute of Education, University of Amsterdam, The Netherlands

Professor Robert L. Thorndike, Teachers College, Columbia University, USA (Chairman).

The National Center in each participating country was requested to set up a national reading committee that could review the proposed plan for the study and could submit and review reading passages and test items.

Initial planning for the study of accomplishment in Reading Comprehension in different countries was undertaken at a meeting of the International Committee in November 1966, and much of the detail was worked out at a week-long meeting in June 1967. After that, operational steps of preparing and reviewing test items and assembling final forms of the test were carried out largely by mail, the work centering on the office of the Committee Chairman.

At the time of its original meeting the International Reading Committee agreed to focus its study of reading upon the cognitive aspects, and not to attempt to assess the aesthetic or affective aspects of reading. The decision was based upon a belief that the aesthetic and stylistic aspects of text would be more difficult to transpose from one language to another than the information content of the text. It was also the case that an International Literature Committee was focusing upon the aesthetics of textual material, so that such an emphasis would have represented duplication of effort.

The original intent of the Committee had been to test both reading comprehension, defined as ability to answer questions about a passage when the passage is available for reference and re-reading, and learning by reading, in which a passage is read and studied and at some subsequent point in time the reader is tested upon what he has comprehended of and remembered from the passage. A third variation was also considered, in which certain general questions are first raised, reading material is presented for study in the light of those questions, and subsequently specific questions are presented, the answers to which are available in the passage. These three were considered to represent the commonest ways in which reading is used in schools. However, practical considerations finally ruled out the latter two types of test. Developmental time was not available to produce and try out all these types of tests, and the schedule of testing time available to administer the tests in schools would not have permitted administration of all types. Testing was limited, therefore, to the first of the three types of test. The examinees were given a reading comprehension test of the conventional type, in which a passage is presented together with multiple-choice questions based upon it, the examinee reads the passage, and then attempts to answer the questions referring back to the passage when and as he finds it necessary.

The comprehension test was supplemented by a brief test of reading speed. The format for this test consisted of a series of short, simple paragraphs, each ending in a multiple-choice question to be marked by the examinee. The primary score for this test was the number of questions attempted. A further supplemental test was a brief test of word knowledge, presented in the form of word pairs, each to be identified as synonyms or antonyms.

At the time that the tests were being planned, a good deal of thought was given to the types of variables that should be studied as predictors of accomplishment in reading. Though these were spoken of at the time as "hypotheses," they are probably more accurately thought of as areas of inquiry. The areas included the following:

1. Out-of-school environment, including home environment, exposure to mass media and compatibility between home language and the language of instruction.

2. Availability of reading materials, including availability in the school, in the home, and in the surrounding community.

3. Educational practices and background, including instructional practices and emphases in the teaching of reading, resources and procedures for individualization of instruction, and size and type of school.

4. The interests and attitudes of the child in relation to reading and to school more generally.

5. Acquired study and reading habits.

6. Presence of or freedom from physical defects, such as defects of eyesight, hearing or speech.

In addition, it was considered to be of interest to examine the relationships among different reading measures, and of the Reading tests with the tests of Literature and Science that were given concurrently.

Chapter 2, which follows immediately, describes the instruments that were actually developed for the project. These include tests to measure accomplishment and questionnaires to gather information about the student, his background and his school. Chapter 3 describes the selection of samples to be tested and the conduct of the testing. The remaining chapters are devoted to an exposition of the results from the survey.

REFERENCES

Foshay, A. W. (Ed.) *Educational Achievements of Thirteen-Year-Olds in Twelve Countries*. Hamburg: Unesco Institute for Education, 1962.

Kumbaraci, Turkan, E. *Translated Reading Tests as Culture-Fair Measures for Foreign Students*. Unpublished doctoral dissertation. New York: Teachers College, Columbia University, 1966.

Development of Instruments for the Study

In order to study reading performance and the factors that are related to that performance in a group of countries it was necessary to prepare both tests to appraise reading abilities of students and questionnaires to gather information of other types from students, teachers and school officials. The development of tests of ability and questionnaires for the collection of background data were two quite separate enterprises, and will be described in separate sections of this chapter. (For further details of the development of the instruments, see Volume VIII of the present series, *An Empirical Study of Education in Twenty-One Countries: A Technical Report.*)

READING TESTS

The first step in developing the reading tests was that of deciding what skills were to be tested. The decisions represented compromises between what might be desirable and what seemed feasible for a large-scale cross-national study. Since the appraisal of reading was to be carried out concurrently with appraisal of achievement in Science and, in some countries, appraisal of achievement in Literature, and since time also had to be provided for questionnaires that would produce information on background variables, it was necessary to place rather tight limits on the time to be devoted to assessing reading capabilities. The realities of large-scale testing also limited the procedures to those that could be administered in groups. Since Literature was being studied separately, and since aesthetic nuances of style seemed the most difficult to preserve from one language to another, it was decided to focus upon the cognitive content of the passage, and to forego most efforts to get at any appraisal of style, feeling, tone or literary techniques. Initially, there had been some thought of testing study-type reading, in which a student studies a fairly extended passage for a time, then puts it aside and is subsequently tested on the content of the passage. However, practical limitations related both to the testing itself and to the preparation of materials led to abandoning this enterprise. As finally conceived, the testing included three components: (1) a reading comprehension test, (2) a reading speed test and (3) a test of word knowledge.

The reading comprehension test was to be of the conventional type in which a passage is presented to the pupil together with multiple-choice questions based on that passage. The examinee reads the passage—and refers back to it as often and as much as he needs to—and then attempts to pick the choice that best answers the question or completes the statement presented in the test exercise. The first step in preparing such a test is the selection of an appropriate passage upon which test exercises can be written. Each National Center was invited to contribute reading passages to a pool from which an eventual selection might be made, and a number did in fact do so. Passages were intensively reviewed by the International Reading Committee at a week-long meeting, and were roughly sorted into seven levels of judged difficulty described as 8-year-old, 10-year-old, 12-year-old, 14-year-old, 16-year-old, 18-year-old, and 18+. The designations represented the age level at which it was judged the passages would be appropriate for the typical student in a country with a high average level of formal education. However, the judgments were intended to represent only a rough preliminary grading of the passages.

A number of passages that seemed to the members of the International Committee to be suitable in style and content, and not to be peculiar to any one culture or country, were selected as possible materials for the test. These passages were reproduced and circulated to all of the countries for comment. Only those passages that were almost universally considered to be acceptable for inclusion were retained for further development. For some passages, a number of test items were already in existence. These were reviewed, and edited where necessary to improve their clarity or to make them conform to a standard four-choice multiple-choice format. Additional items were written for almost all passages and in those cases in which no test items were available a complete set was prepared. A considerable surplus of items was prepared for each passage to allow for attrition during review at the national level and during try-out. These items were subsequently sent to all national committees for comments and suggestions and for the supplying of additional items wherever a national committee cared to make such a contribution to the enterprise.

Taking account of the comments and suggestions of national committees, and including items provided by these groups wherever possible, six try-out test forms were prepared for each of the populations to be included in the IEA study, to wit, 10-year-olds, 14-year-olds, and students in the final year of secondary education. Each 10-year-old try-out test included three passages, one that had been rated as an 8-year-old passage, one a 10-year-old passage, and one a 12-year-old passage. The try-out tests for Population II (14-year-olds) contained four passages spanning the 12-, 14-, and 16-year-old levels. The end-of-secondary test also included four passages, but at the 16, 18, and 18+ levels. Thus, the test at each level had one passage in common with the next level. All told, 50 different passages and 445 different items were tried out. From among these, 20 passages and 131 items were eventually selected for use in the main study.

Test development was carried out during 1967, and tests were distributed for try-out around March 1968. Try-outs were completed before the end of the 1967–1968 school year. The amount of material to be translated and tried out was more than could have been handled in any one country, so the six forms of the tests were divided into three sets of two forms each, and each participating country was asked to pretest one third of the material. The schedule called for each test to be tried out in four countries, one an English-speaking country and the other three each representing a different language. It was hoped that in this way each test would have been pretested in enough different languages to make it possible to eliminate items that were discriminating in only one or two languages, and that the items that were retained would prove to be discriminating in the remaining languages as well as in those in which they were tried out. For most tests, data for four countries were available as planned, but difficulties arose in relation to some of the try-outs so that a few passages were tried out in only two or three countries. It was intended that each passage be tried out on a sample of two or three hundred in each country in which data were collected, but samples were in some cases smaller than that.

Analysis of its try-out data was carried out by each National Center that had participated in the pretesting, and the results were sent in to be centrally collated for each of the reading passages. The collated data were circulated for review by the International Reading Committee, and on the basis of recommendations received from the

Table 2.1. *Distribution of Item Difficulty Indices by Population and Country for Reading Comprehension Test. Population I*

% Correct	Belgium (Fl)	Belgium (Fr)	Chile	England	Finland	Hungary	India
90–99	1	—	—	—	1	1	—
80–89	4	4	1	1	4	1	1
70–79	5	7	—	8	6	2	—
60–69	8	8	1	10	11	8	3
50–59	6	6	6	8	5	10	5
40–49	6	7	9	10	10	8	12
30–39	10	6	16	7	3	5	13
20–29	3	5	11	1	5	7	7
10–19	2	2	1	—	—	3	4
Median	53.7	55.6	36.9	56.4	59.1	49.1	37.4

Table 2.1. *Population I (Cont.)*

% Correct	Iran	Israel	Italy	Netherlands	Scotland	Sweden	United States	Grand Total
90–99	—	—	1	1	—	—	—	5
80–89	—	1	5	2	2	6	1	33
70–79	—	1	13	9	6	10	4	71
60–69	—	8	6	6	10	9	10	98
50–59	3	9	5	9	10	8	11	101
40–49	6	13	6	5	8	4	9	113
30–39	10	5	6	8	7	5	6	107
20–29	15	2	3	3	2	3	3	70
10–19	11	6	—	2	—	—	1	32
Median	27.8	47.4	64.1	55.4	56.2	62.4	53.4	49.4

members the test editor made a final selection of passages and items.

Passages were selected to provide a suitable range of difficulty for the population in question. A second consideration in selection of passages was the number and diversity of items showing suitable difficulty and discrimination. Finally, the attempt was made to get variety of content and treatment. Items were retained that showed acceptable difficulty and discrimination indices, and within these limits an attempt was made to include items covering as wide a range of reading skills as possible, i.e., items dealing with specific factual

Table 2.1. *Population II*

% Correct	Belgium (Fl)	Belgium (Fr)	Chile	Eng- land	Fin- land	Hun- gary	India	Iran
90–99	4	4	—	1	1	1	—	—
80–89	7	13	—	8	9	9	—	—
70–79	7	7	3	9	10	11	—	4
60-69	7	5	8	10	12	9	4	2
50–59	11	7	9	12	10	5	4	1
40–49	5	10	10	5	6	9	2	9
30–39	5	4	10	3	2	6	16	11
20–29	5	1	11	4	1	2	17	17
10–19	1	—	1	—	1	—	7	7
0-9	—	1	—	—	—	—	2	1
Median	58.7	66.6	45.7	61.6	64.2	65.0	30.0	31.0

Table 2.1. *Population II* (*Cont.*)

% Correct	Israel	Italy	Nether- lands	New Zealand	Scot- land	Sweden	United States	Grand Total
90–99	—	7	1	3	3	1	2	28
80–89	5	8	10	13	9	12	9	112
70–79	8	7	9	10	9	11	11	116
60–69	10	8	8	11	11	4	10	119
50–59	11	9	8	6	9	10	9	121
40–49	12	7	7	5	4	5	6	102
30–39	3	2	4	1	3	3	2	75
20–29	2	4	5	3	4	6	2	84
10–19	1	—	—	—	—	—	1	19
0–9	—	—	—	—	—	—	—	4
Median	57.4	64.0	65.0	70.0	65.8	65.0	66.6	58.7

details, with the main idea, with inference beyond the literal content of the passage, with the author's point of view and purpose, and with the author's writing techniques.

Final tests were prepared as follows: for Population I (10-year-olds) two tests each planned to have a time allowance of 25 minutes, each composed of four passages and including jointly a total of 45 items; for Population II (14-year-olds) two tests each planed to have a time allowance of 45 minutes, including jointly eight passages and a total of 52 items; and for Population IV (end of secondary

Table 2.1. *Population IV*

% Correct	Belgium (Fl)	Belgium (Fr)	Chile	England	Finland	Hungary	India	Iran
90–99	1	3	—	5	4	2	—	—
80–89	4	6	—	15	15	6	—	—
70–79	15	11	7	11	10	10	—	—
60–69	7	9	5	8	8	11	—	—
50–59	13	12	9	9	5	7	3	3
40–49	5	6	13	3	1	3	3	8
30–39	3	4	8	2	6	8	17	13
20–29	4	2	8	1	4	6	19	17
10–19	1	1	3	—	1	1	12	11
0–9	1	—	1	—	—	—	—	2
Median	60.0	65.6	43.8	75.0	72.0	61.6	27.1	27.8

Table 2.1. *Population IV (Cont.)*

% Correct	Israel	Italy	Netherlands	New Zealand	Scotland	Sweden	United States	Grand Total
90–99	1	2	11	8	7	4	1	49
80–89	6	7	10	18	15	6	3	111
70–79	15	11	9	7	11	10	8	135
60–69	9	4	7	12	11	7	8	106
50–59	7	14	3	4	5	10	11	115
40–49	5	5	6	1	1	12	15	87
30–39	5	4	2	3	3	2	3	83
20–29	5	4	4	1	1	2	5	83
10–19	1	2	2	—	—	1	—	36
0–9	—	1	—	—	—	—	—	5
Median	62.8	58.3	73.0	78.3	76.8	60.0	56.1	59.6

school) two tests each planned to have a time allowance of 50 minutes, including jointly eight passages and a total of 54 items.

Some sense of the statistical properties of the resulting tests can be obtained from Tables 2.1 and 2.2. Table 2.1 shows the distribution of item difficulties, expressed as percent getting the item right, for each country at each level, i.e., 10-year-olds, 14-year-olds and end of secondary education. Table 2.2 shows the item discrimination indices, expressed as point-biserial correlation between item and total score on the test, by country and level. Median difficulties and dis-

Table 2.2. *Distribution of Item Discrimination Indices (Point Biserial Correlations) by Population and Country for Reading Comprehension Test. Population I*

Discrimination index	Belgium (Fl)	Belgium (Fr)	Chile	England	Finland	Hungary	India
.60–.69	—	1	—	1	2	—	—
.50–.59	4	3	7	14	7	6	8
.40–.49	10	14	11	11	16	13	10
.30–.39	16	14	11	12	12	14	9
.20–.29	11	8	9	4	4	4	9
.10–.19	2	1	3	3	4	5	6
.00–.09	2	4	3	—	—	3	1
Negative	—	—	1	—	—	—	2
Median	.34	.38	.37	.42	.41	.37	.36

Table 2.2. *Population I (Cont.)*

Discrimination index	Iran	Israel	Italy	Netherlands	Scotland	Sweden	United States	Grand total
.60–.69	—	1	—	—	—	—	—	5
.50–.59	—	13	4	7	11	10	11	105
.40–.49	3	12	21	9	13	15	17	175
.30–.39	20	8	9	16	11	10	9	171
.20–.29	10	5	5	6	7	6	6	94
.10–.19	7	5	5	4	2	4	2	53
.00–.09	4	—	—	3	1	—	—	21
Negative	1	1	1	—	—	—	—	6
Median	.30	.45	.41	.37	.41	.42	.43	.38

crimination indices are shown, calculated from a finer grouping of item difficulties and discrimination than finally reported in these tables.

The test items showed a wide spread of difficulty. Median percent of correct answers, pooling the results for all countries, was 49.4 for Population I, 58.7 for Population II and 59.6 for Population IV. For Population I the test appears to have been somewhat too hard, but for the other two populations the difficulty was about what one would wish to obtain for effective measurement. However, in the three developing countries (Chile, India and Iran) the test

25

Table 2.2. *Population II*

Discrimination index	Belgium (Fl)	Belgium (Fr)	Chile	England	Finland	Hungary	India	Iran
.50–.59	1	1	5	6	2	—	—	—
.40–.49	11	8	11	23	12	9	2	—
.30–.39	19	16	14	15	28	25	17	12
.20–.29	17	19	18	4	8	12	15	21
.10–.19	3	7	4	2	2	6	11	15
.00–.09	—	—	—	2	—	—	6	3
Negative	1	1	—	—	—	—	1	1
Median	.33	.29	.32	.41	.36	.33	.24	.23

Table 2.2. *Population II* (*Cont.*)

Discrimination index	Israel	Italy	Netherlands	New Zealand	Scotland	Sweden	United States	Grand total
.50–.59	11	—	—	5	6	4	6	47
.40–.49	15	9	13	16	19	14	19	181
.30–.39	19	20	23	22	17	21	17	285
.20–.29	5	18	11	6	7	10	6	177
.10–.09	2	5	4	3	2	1	3	70
.00–.09	—	—	1	—	1	2	1	16
Negative	—	—	—	—	—	—	—	4
Median	.40	.32	.34	.38	.39	.36	.39	.34

tasks were clearly too difficult. In some instances the median percent of correct responses fell only slightly above what might have been expected by chance for four-choice multiple-choice items, which, however, does not imply that guessing was more frequent in these countries.

In general, the items discriminated satisfactorily between good and poor readers. The overall median of the point-biserial correlations between item and total test was 0.38 for Population I, 0.34 for Population II, and 0.29 for Population IV. The drop, especially that at Population IV, can be attributed at least in part to the greater homogeneity in ability of those who have survived to the end of secondary education. Discrimination indices averaged a little higher

Table 2.2. *Population IV*

Discrimination index	Belgium (Fl)	Belgium (Fr)	Chile	England	Finland	Hungary	India	Iran
.50–.59	—	—	—	1	—	—	—	—
.40–.49	8	9	3	6	3	4	1	1
.30–.39	17	16	21	24	15	23	5	13
.20–.29	19	21	17	16	24	17	18	19
.10–.19	7	7	9	6	10	7	21	11
.00–.09	2	1	4	1	2	3	8	8
Negative	1	—	—	—	—	—	1	2
Median	.29	.29	.29	.32	.26	.30	.18	.22

Table 2.2. *Population IV (Cont.)*

Discrimination index	Israel	Italy	Netherlands	New Zealand	Scotland	Sweden	United States	Grand total
.50–.59	8	—	—	—	—	—	7	16
.40–.49	12	17	3	5	5	9	14	100
.30–.39	11	20	14	20	19	21	20	259
.20–.29	14	7	24	18	20	16	9	259
.10–.19	8	4	11	10	8	6	2	127
.00–.09	—	4	2	1	2	1	—	39
Negative	1	2	—	—	—	1	2	10
Median	.36	.37	.26	.29	.28	.31	.36	.29

than the median for English-speaking countries. Editorial and developmental work on the items was carried out in English, and all items were tried out in an English-speaking country. It is gratifying that the discriminating ability of the items held up with little deterioration in languages other than English. The only countries showing seriously reduced discrimination were those developing countries in which the test tasks appeared to be clearly too difficult.

Persons writing about reading abilities and the teaching of reading have tended to recognize and be concerned with a number of more or less distinct skills. Such skills as identifying the main idea of a paragraph, finding the answer to a question specifically answered in the passage, recognizing something implied by the passage but not specifically stated, and identifying the writer's purpose or point of view have frequently been mentioned. In selecting items for the present tests, the Committee attempted to have representation of a wide range of these skills. A limited analysis was made of subscores, each designed to represent some one of these skills. Classification of items into the specific skill groupings was based on the judgment of several experts at Teachers College, Columbia University, and is admittedly subjective and somewhat unreliable. The subscores turned out to have little uniqueness, as will be pointed out in Chapter 4, and only limited use was made of them.

The original rationale for the reading appraisal included a proposal to assess reading speed as well as reading comprehension, since speed is a relatively independent aspect of reading skill that has some importance as an academic accomplishment. Assessment of reading speed has always presented a number of technical problems and no fully satisfactory technique for this type of assessment has been developed. One wishes to retain a natural reading situation; one wishes some guarantee that the material has indeed been read and understood; and at the same time one wishes to assess maximum speed of comprehension. Various possible testing patterns were considered. The one that was finally used is a pattern that has appeared in widely-used reading tests in several countries to assess speed of reading. This procedure involves providing a series of relatively short paragraphs, each of which ends with a question and is followed by three words, one of which is to be underlined as answering the question. A paragraph might read:

"Peter has three dogs. One is black and the others are brown. How many brown dogs does Peter have?

one   two   three"

The paragraphs have to be constructed in such a way that the most economical and efficient way of answering is to read the whole paragraph, rather than reading merely the question. When this is the case, the process is a reasonably natural one of reading a sentence or two followed by a question and then responding to that question.

In the materials that were prepared for this purpose in the IEA study, the sequence of paragraphs constituted a single continuous story. The attempt was made to write the material at a very low level of difficulty, so that the measure would be that of the fluency in mechanics of reading material of a very simple nature. Two stories were prepared and were distributed to the national groups for comment and subsequently for try-out. The materials were administered for try-out with the instruction for each child to read as rapidly as he could, while still getting the information needed to answer the questions. The child was instructed to mark clearly where he was at the end of three minutes and again at the end of six minutes so that it would be possible to get two distributions of items attempted and provide two marks to guide the final decision as to the optimal testing time.

In addition to getting data on the timing of the passages in the preliminary try-out, each country was asked to tally the number of errors on each of the items in the stories so that items that were ambiguous or too difficult could be identified and modified. It turned out that one story had a number of rather ambiguous items and items that presented difficulty to children whereas the other had relatively very few. On this basis, the second story was chosen for the final testing and was edited to try to minimize those difficulties that were in fact found in it. The first story was also edited to eliminate as much as possible of the ambiguity and difficulty, with the intention that it would be used as a practice story. On the basis of the try-out, a time limit of four minutes was set for a passage consisting of 40 items like the one shown above.

Answers for the reading speed test were marked directly on the test booklet. This procedure made for substantial practical difficulties in scoring the test. It might have been desirable to check the correctness of all the answers on this simple material. However, this represented an unduly burdensome clerical task. As a compromise, two scores were obtained. One was simply the number of the last item attempted, without regard to the correctness of any item. The other was an error score based on the first page (the first nine items) of the test. The resulting measure of accuracy of comprehension of the speeded material, though relatively unreliable, provided an additional score that could be combined in whatever way seemed desirable with the simple speed score.

A third component that was proposed in the original plan for the reading test was a test of word knowledge. This was seen less as an inherent part of the reading test than as a control variable on verbal ability that might be useful and relevant in relation to all the tests of the IEA study.

As something of a *tour de force,* the editor for the reading test undertook to try to produce a common test to be used across languages in all of the different participating countries, and to be of comparable difficulty in each language.

The item format that was selected was that of word pairs where the words of a pair must be judged to be approximately either synonyms or antonyms, that is, either nearly the same in meaning or nearly the opposite in meaning. It was thought that this item format would be easier to translate into different languages than the conventional multiple-choice format with a number of wrong options. Here it was felt that the attractiveness of wrong options would vary so much from country to country that it would be extremely difficult to get items equivalent from one language to another.

In order to accumulate a pool of items that might be used for this study, national committees in each country were invited to submit sets of word pairs ranging from easy to difficult, providing them to the editor in their English translation. A list of some 300 word pairs was assembled. The difficulty of these in English was judged by several experts at Teachers College, and the words were arranged into ten classes with respect to their judged difficulty. The set of words was then circulated to each of the national committees, and each committee was asked to indicate which of the pairs it would be either impossible or difficult to translate into a pair of corresponding difficulty in the language of the country.

The data from the above assessments were assembled and tabulated, and all word pairs were dropped from further study in which more than one country indicated difficulty in the matter of translation. The remaining word pairs were assembled into three try-out tests, one for 10-year-olds, one for 14-year-olds, and one for end of secondary school students, and were circulated to the participating countries for try-out in their school systems. Some of the items in adjacent tests were common to permit scaling items from successive test levels on a common scale.

The original hope and plan in designing the vocabulary test was that there would be among the rather large pool of items tried out a subset of items that were of comparable difficulty from one country to another. The problem becomes one of defining comparable difficulty in different countries using different types of samples and different languages. The assumption on which the attempt to scale difficulty across countries was based was that *on the average for the whole pool of items* they would be about equally difficult in English and in the language into which they were being translated. The subsidiary expectation was that the correlation of item difficulty from one language to another would be positive and fairly high, though obviously far from perfect.

Data were reported to IEA in the form of percent passing a given item. In some countries, item vs. test correlations were also reported, making it possible to identify items that were not differentiating between the more and the less able pupils.

Items were scaled for difficulty, first within each age sample of a country, then across age samples for that country, and then in relation to the United States as a common anchor population. The sequence of steps is outlined below:

1. Proportion "knowing" an item was defined as proportion correct minus proportion wrong (R − W),

2. The proportion established in (1) was converted into a deviation score on the baseline of a normal curve,

3. Using those words that were common to the Population I and Population II tests, the difference in means and the ratio of standard deviations in the two groups were estimated,

4. Scale scores for the Population II items were converted to the Population I scale by the appropriate linear equation,

5. In the same manner, Population IV scale values were converted to Population II and finally to Population I scale values,

6. Scale values as determined in (5) for Country X were plotted against United States scale values, and the means, standard deviations, and intercorrelations computed, and

7. A conversion equation was applied to the Country X data to produce the same mean and standard deviation as those for the United States.

As the data were received and examined, it seemed rather doubtful whether either of the original expectations, i.e. of equal average difficulty for the complete set or of high correlation of difficulties from one language to another, was borne out. In particular, there were a number of the translation languages in which the items showed a very limited spread of difficulty. Generally speaking, the range of difficulty was greater in English than it was in the languages into which the words were translated and this kind of a regression towards mediocrity was larger in some languages than in others.

It also appeared that the items tended to get systematically easier in translation, though this could not be tested in any rigorous sense because little was known about the comparability of the try-out samples from the different countries. It certainly did appear that the items that had been very difficult in English lapsed into being

Table 2.3. *Distribution of Item Difficulty Indices by Population and Country for Word Knowledge Test. Population I*

% Correct	Belgium (Fl)	Belgium (Fr)	Chile	England	FRG	Finland	Hungary	India
90–99	7	5	1	3	—	11	5	—
80–89	12	11	2	3	5	11	11	2
70–79	7	12	10	9	10	5	14	4
60–69	6	5	10	13	9	4	6	11
50–59	5	5	10	8	4	3	3	9
40–49	3	1	5	4	8	2	1	12
30–39	—	1	2	—	1	—	—	2
20–29	—	—	—	—	2	—	—	—
10–19	—	—	—	—	1	3	—	—
0–9	—	—	—	—	—	1	—	—
Median	78.3	76.6	61.8	66.8	66.4	81.4	77.7	56.2

Table 2.3. *Population I (Cont.)*

% Correct	Iran	Israel	Italy	Netherlands	Scotland	Sweden	United States	Grand total
90–99	—	—	13	5	3	4	3	60
80–89	—	3	17	7	2	7	6	99
70–79	9	10	7	5	10	7	8	127
60–69	10	12	3	9	7	9	15	129
50–59	10	6	—	8	11	0	6	88
40–49	7	4	—	5	6	8	2	68
30–39	3	4	—	—	1	3	—	17
20–29	1	—	—	1	—	1	—	5
10–19	—	1	—	—	—	1	—	6
0–9	—	—	—	—	—	—	—	1
Median	59.2	65.6	86.4	67.2	63.3	65.0	68.3	68.9

only moderately difficult in many of the translations, and that there were relatively few instances of the reverse, where an item that had been only moderately difficult in English became very difficult in one of the other languages. Furthermore, the average correlation of item difficulty from language to language, even including a range of words from those that were quite easy for 10-year-olds to those that were quite difficult for pupils at the end of secondary school (in English in any event), was only about 0.4 or 0.5. As a result, there was very large scattering of difficulty indices for an item, and

Table 2.3. *Population II*

% Correct	Australia	Belgium (Fl)	Belgium (Fr)	Chile	England	FRG	Finland	Hungary	India
90–99	3	16	10	—	—	1	2	17	—
80–89	8	10	8	6	9	11	8	15	—
70–79	7	6	7	5	5	5	8	5	2
60–69	4	3	9	8	9	3	11	2	9
50–59	8	4	3	11	9	8	5	—	16
40–49	6	1	3	9	2	6	3	—	8
30–39	3	—	—	1	6	3	3	1	5
20–29	1	—	—	—	—	3	—	—	—
10–19	—	—	—	—	—	—	—	—	—
0–9	—	—	—	—	—	—	—	—	—
Median	65.0	87.4	76.6	58.7	62.4	60.0	67.4	88.1	54.3

Table 2.3. *Population II (Cont.)*

% Correct	Iran	Israel	Italy	Netherlands	New Zealand	Scotland	Sweden	United States	Grand total
90–99	6	1	17	6	5	2	6	8	100
80–89	9	13	9	13	9	9	5	6	148
70–79	10	8	7	5	4	6	3	6	99
60–69	3	8	3	5	5	7	9	4	102
50–59	7	6	2	3	7	8	7	10	114
40–49	4	2	—	3	7	3	8	2	67
30–39	—	1	—	3	3	5	2	4	40
20–29	1	1	—	2	—	—	—	—	8
10–19	—	—	—	—	—	—	—	—	—
0–9	—	—	2	—	—	—	—	—	2
Median	74.1	73.3	85.0	79.0	66.6	63.3	63.7	65.0	70.8

it was hard to find a subset of items that were very nearly the same in difficulty across all languages. An attempt was made to select the best subset possible in the sense that items were chosen to try to balance difficulty from one language to another and items were chosen where the spread of difficulties across languages was relatively small compared with others of the items. However, it must be admitted that the final result is one in which the equivalence from language to language is suspect.

Tests consisting of 40 items were prepared for each of the three

Table 2.3. *Population IV*

% Correct	Australia	Belgium (Fl)	Belgium (Fr)	Chile	England	FRG	Finland	France	Hungary
90–99	7	19	20	6	14	14	6	21	30
80–89	9	11	13	10	7	5	8	11	9
70–79	8	2	4	10	8	7	7	4	—
60–69	7	2	3	6	3	6	3	3	—
50–59	5	1	—	6	6	2	6	—	—
40–49	3	2	—	2	1	3	2	1	—
30–39	1	2	—	—	1	1	2	—	1
20–29	—	—	—	—	—	1	3	—	—
10–19	—	—	—	—	—	1	2	—	—
0–9	—	1	—	—	—	—	1	—	—
Median	76.0	89.1	90.0	76.6	81.6	77.4	71.0	90.5	95.2

Table 2.3. *Population IV* (*Cont.*)

% Correct	India	Iran	Israel	Italy	Netherlands	New Zealand	Scotland	Sweden	United States	Grand total
90–99	—	8	7	32	22	11	12	15	1	245
80–89	2	15	7	5	8	9	10	7	3	149
70–79	3	6	12	1	3	10	5	9	11	110
60–69	14	4	2	1	4	4	6	2	11	80
50–59	11	4	6	1	—	5	6	3	7	69
40–49	6	2	1	—	1	1	—	3	5	33
30–39	4	—	1	—	1	—	1	1	2	18
20–29	—	—	2	—	1	—	—	—	—	7
10–19	—	1	1	1	—	—	—	—	—	6
0–9	—	—	1	—	—	—	—	—	—	3
Median	59.0	82.4	74.2	95.0	91.1	80.0	81.4	83.3	64.2	82.3

levels—10-year-olds, 14-year-olds and end of secondary school. In order to permit some comparison of performance from one group to the next, 13 items were common to the tests for Populations I and II, 21 to the tests for Populations II and IV. Distributions of item difficulty and item discrimination indices for the word knowledge test are shown in Tables 2.3 and 2.4 respectively. In Population I a good spread of item difficulties was obtained in all countries except Italy, where the items seemed to be generally quite easy. Once again, percentages correct tended to be low in the developing

Table 2.4. *Distribution of Item Discrimination Indices (Point-Biserial Correlations) by Population and Country for Word Knowledge Test. Population I*

Discrimination index	Belgium (Fl)	Belgium (Fr)	Chile	England	FRG	Finland	Hungary	India
.60–.69	—	—	1	—	—	—	—	—
.50–.59	1	2	11	7	—	7	8	10
.40–.49	9	12	18	18	10	12	22	20
.30–.39	19	18	10	11	18	14	7	6
.20–.29	6	6	—	4	8	1	1	4
.10–.19	3	2	—	—	2	2	2	—
.00–.09	2	—	—	—	—	—	—	—
Negative	—	—	—	—	2	4	—	—
Median	.36	.37	.46	.44	.36	.39	.45	.45

Table 2.4. *Population I (Cont.)*

Discrimination index	Iran	Israel	Italy	Netherlands	Scotland	Sweden	United States	Grand total
.60–.69	1	—	—	—	—	—	—	2
.50–.59	11	7	3	—	2	—	—	69
.40–.49	13	17	23	9	19	7	13	222
.30–.39	6	9	12	18	15	15	19	197
.20–.29	6	2	2	9	3	11	6	69
.10–.19	2	—	—	2	1	4	2	22
.00–.09	1	3	—	2	—	2	—	10
Negative	—	2	—	—	—	1	—	9
Median	.45	.44	.42	.33	.41	.32	.37	.40

countries. (It must be remembered that with these two-choice items 50% of correct answers could be expected to arise as a result of random guessing.) In Population II the items appeared to be generally easy in Flemish-speaking Belgium, in Hungary and in Italy, while at Population IV France, French-speaking Belgium and the Netherlands must be added to the list. The variation from country to country for this test appears to be clearly much greater than for the reading comprehension test.

In spite of the rather wide variation from country to country in

Table 2.4. *Population II*

Discrimination index	Australia	Belgium (Fl)	Belgium (Fr)	Chile	England	FRG	Finland	Hungary	India
.60–.69	—	—	2	—	—	—	—	—	—
.50–.59	—	—	3	2	1	1	—	1	—
.40–.49	13	13	8	17	17	16	6	27	8
.30–.39	15	17	14	16	12	19	17	8	23
.20–.29	12	9	10	4	9	2	10	2	7
.10–.19	—	1	3	1	1	2	6	2	1
.00–.09	—	—	—	—	—	—	1	—	1
Negative	—	—	—	—	—	—	—	—	—
Median	.36	.36	.36	.39	.39	.39	.32	.43	.35

Table 2.4. *Population II* (*Cont.*)

Discrimination index	Iran	Israel	Italy	Netherlands	New Zealand	Scotland	Sweden	United States	Grand total
.60–.69	—	1	—	—	—	—	—	—	3
.50–.59	1	6	—	—	—	—	—	—	15
.40–.49	13	13	13	8	14	13	3	2	204
.30–.39	16	14	20	20	18	16	15	23	283
.20–.29	8	4	5	6	7	10	13	11	129
.10–.19	1	1	—	4	1	1	8	4	37
.00–.09	1	—	—	1	—	—	1	—	5
Negative	—	1	2	1	—	—	—	—	4
Median	.37	.40	.37	.34	.37	.37	.29	.32	.36

difficulty, the items showed rather good and relatively consistent discrimination within each country. Thus, it appears that the test should be a reasonably satisfactory measure of verbal ability for *within-country* analyses. It would only become suspect if it were used for cross-language comparisons.

QUESTIONNAIRES

The other main section of the data gathering was based on questionnaires to be completed by each student tested, by a sample of teachers in each school, and by an administrative representative for

Table 2.4. *Population IV*

Discri-mination index	Aus-tralia	Belgium (Fl)	Belgium (Fr)	Chile	Eng-land	FRG	Fin-land	France	Hun-gary
.50–.59	—	—	3	1	—	4	—	—	—
.40–.49	5	4	9	17	7	9	2	10	5
.30–.39	19	19	10	18	16	11	11	14	15
.20–.29	9	14	17	4	14	6	22	11	19
.10–.19	7	2	1	—	3	7	4	5	1
.00–.09	—	—	—	—	—	3	1	—	—
Negative	—	1	—	—	—	—	—	—	—
Median	.33	.31	.32	.37	.33	.35	.27	.32	.30

Table 2.4. *Population IV* (*Cont.*)

Discri-mination index	India	Iran	Is-rael	Italy	Nether-lands	New Zealand	Scot-land	Swe-den	United States	Grand total
.50–.59	—	—	5	6	—	—	—	—	—	19
.40–.49	4	6	14	13	3	8	5	3	2	126
.30–.39	23	20	6	14	15	22	15	19	23	290
.20–.29	8	11	8	6	13	6	16	14	13	211
.10–.19	5	2	4	—	9	4	4	4	2	64
.00–.09	—	—	—	—	—	—	—	—	—	4
Negative	—	1	3	1	—	—	—	—	—	6
Median	.34	.32	.35	.39	.28	.33	.30	.31	.32	.32

the school. Items to be included in the questionnaires were submitted by each of the subject matter committees and by a more general committee concerned with hypotheses to be investigated in the six subject study. These were reviewed by a special questionnaire committee and divided into questions of general interest to all subject matters and those of special interest to a single subject area.

Some of the questions (such as one to determine sex) were of a sort for which the options were obvious. There were others, however, (such as one concerned with hours of homework per week) for which it was difficult to tell in advance what range of responses would be received and how these should be divided into response categories in a precoded questionnaire. In order to guide the choice, a number of the items were pretested in open-ended form. Frequency distributions of responses were prepared for the several countries in which the try-out had been conducted, and these were used as a basis for setting up response categories. For example, on a question asking about hours per week reading for pleasure, it appeared that a good spread of responses within and between countries would result from choices as follows:

0 hours
Less than 1 hour
Between 1 and 2 hours
Between 2 and 3 hours
More than 3 hours.

The same coding was used for all countries, and sometimes represented a compromise that was far from ideal for single countries in the study.

After the preliminary try-out, the members of the questionnaire committee carried out a final review and selection of questions. The review was designed to keep the questionnaires to manageable size in view of demands upon student and teacher time, to phrase the questions so that they would be as clear and simple as possible, to provide suitable precoded response alternatives whenever this was possible, and to provide open-ended responses that would be easy to code in those instances in which precoding was not practical.

The preliminary forms of the questionnaires were circulated to National Centers for review and were revised on the basis of suggestions from this source. Final forms were then prepared and distributed for translation and use.

Some questions suggested by, or of special interest to the International Reading Committee are listed below. Other questions are described in later chapters, in relation to their use in the statistical analysis.

STUDENT QUESTIONNAIRE

13. How often is a dictionary used by anyone in your home? (check one)
    Often
    Occasionally
    Never, or do not have one

16. Does your family receive a *daily* newspaper? (Check one)

    Yes

    No, but I read one most days anyway

    No, and I never read one

17. About how many hours do you usually watch TV on a *school day,* outside of school programs?

    . . . . . hours

18. About how many books are there in your home? (Do not count newspapers or magazines) (check one)

    None . . . . .

    1–10 . . . . .

    11–25 . . . . .

    26–50 . . . . .

    51 or more . . . . .

19. About how many hours did you spend reading for your own pleasure last week? (not including comics) (check one)

    0 hours . . . . .

    Less than 1 hour . . . . .

    Between 1 and 2 hours . . . . .

    Between 2 and 3 hours . . . . .

    More than 3 hours . . . . .

TEACHER QUESTIONNAIRE

Directions: In questions 2 through 6, please indicate how many weeks (full-time equivalent) of in-service teacher training you have received during the last 5 years in each of the following subjects. Please also include evening courses and other short in-service courses, counting 6 hours equal to one full-time day and 5 days equal to one full-time week.

3. In teaching skills of reading:

    A. 0 weeks

    B. Less than 2 weeks

    C. Between 2 and 4 weeks

    D. Between 4 and 9 weeks

    E. More than 9 weeks.

7. Do you schedule any periods in which students are allowed to spend time reading materials of their own choice?
   A. Yes
   B. No

8. How do your students obtain their reading textbooks?
   A. Buy their own
   B. Loaned to them
   C. Do not have one

9. Does each student have a dictionary exclusively for himself for class use?
   A. Yes
   B. No

10. Is there a class library or book corner in the classroom in which you most often teach?
    A. Yes
    B. No

11. If your answer to question 10 was *yes*, indicate how many books there are in this classroom library or book corner.
    A. Less than 10
    B. Between 10 and 20
    C. Between 20 and 50
    D. Between 50 and 100
    E. More than 100

12. If your answer to question 10 was *yes*, indicate about how many books have been added in the last year.
    A. Less than 10
    B. Between 10 and 20
    C. Between 20 and 30
    D. Between 30 and 40
    E. More than 40

14. About how many clock hours of pre-service training have you had in methods of teaching reading?
    A. None
    B. Between 1 and 10 hours
    C. More than 10 hours

15. Has a standardized reading test (i.e., one which refers students' scores to national or regional norms) been given to all children in your class during the last twelve months?
    A. Yes
    B. No

16. Do you give individual instruction in reading to children in your class?
    A. Yes
    B. No

17. Do you divide the class into groups for instruction in reading?
    A. Yes
    B. No

18. Do you often ask groups of students to read aloud?
    A. Yes
    B. No

19. Do you often read aloud to the students with the students just listening?
    A. Yes
    B. No

20. Do you often read aloud with the students following silently in their own texts?
    A. Yes
    B. No

21. Do you undertake any special work to improve the student's *rate* of reading?
    A. Yes
    B. No

37. *Within a classroom,* teachers sometimes organize students into small instructional groups according to whether they are fast, medium or slow learners. To what extent do you practice such *within class* grouping? (Choose one)
    A. Always or almost always
    B. Frequently
    C. Occasionally
    D. Rarely or never.

34. Indicate approximately how many persons in each of the following positions (full-time equivalent) provide a service in this school according to the following code: 0 = None; 1 = One; 2 = Two; 3 = Three; 4 = Four; 5 = Five; 6 = Six or more.

. . . . . School librarian
. . . . . Laboratory assistant or technician
. . . . . School counsellor
. . . . . School psychologist
. . . . . Reading specialist
. . . . . Social worker
. . . . . Teacher aide
. . . . . Foreign language assistant

35. Do you have available to your school any specialist service (e.g. a child guidance clinic or a school psychological service) to which students with reading difficulties can be referred?

1. Yes
2. No

40. Indicate what provision, if any, the school has for remedial teaching or tutoring in each of the following subject areas according to the following code: 1 = No provision is made; 2 = In cases of great need only; 3 = Generally available

. . . . . Mathematics
. . . . . Science
. . . . . Reading
. . . . . English

The limitations of questionnaire procedures for obtaining information about pupils, teachers and schools must be acknowledged. Limitations of two types should be considered. On the one hand, responses may not be accurate. On the other hand, the items of information may provide only an incomplete and often indirect indication of the phenomenon in which one is interested.

Concern for accuracy of response becomes most acute in relation to the 10-year-olds. A child's answer might be inaccurate because he could not really read and understand the question. It might be inaccurate because he did not have or could not remember the desired information. Thus, he might have only a rough idea of what work his father did. It might be inaccurate because he was unable to make the quantitative synthesis and judgment called for, as, for example, in estimating an average amount of time spent in free reading.

Some preliminary studies were made of accuracy of responding by the child, using factual items and checking his responses against information from independent sources. Results from these studies were generally encouraging, but it must be recognized that the studies did not focus specifically upon those children who had difficulty with reading nor upon those countries where reading skills were least well developed. It is still possible that for such situations the questionnaire responses are quite undependable.

In the Teacher and School Questionnaires, the limitations appeared to focus more on the relevance of the bits of information that it was possible to obtain to the issues that one wishes to study. Thus, one thing that one might like to know is how adequately a school had diagnosed individual differences in reading progress and adapted instruction to those differences. But specific questions to current teachers concerning standardized testing, grouping for reading instruction, and individual tutoring, and to the school concerning grouping policies, provision of resource personnel for diagnostic and remedial work, and so forth give only a spotty and indirect picture of how much had been done and almost no clue as to how well it had been done.

Thus, all in all one must view the questionnaire data with a healthy scepticism and recognize that they represent an incomplete and less than precise picture both of individual children and of schools.

Chapter 3

Selecting the Samples and Administering the Tests

This chapter will be devoted to procedures and problems of two sorts. First we will consider the matter of obtaining the samples of students to be tested for the study, and then we will consider the actual testing procedures and the administrative arrangements that were required to carry out the testing. (See also the *Technical Report* referred to above.)

SAMPLING

For this study, as had been noted earlier, three student populations were defined from which samples were to be drawn. Population I was defined as 10-year-olds, Population II as 14-year-olds, and Population IV as students in the final year of secondary education. Of course, as will be elaborated somewhat further presently, the populations were limited to individuals actually in school, and no attempt was made to get those members of an age group who for one reason or another had never been in or had dropped out of schooling. It was expected that at the two lower levels in the developed countries almost all members of the age group would be in school, because these ages fell within the limits of legal compulsory education for most of the countries involved. However, of course, there are always some individuals who are not able to attend school, and these were not included among the populations to be tested.

In a survey study such as the present one, it is particularly important that one obtain representative samples of the populations that are to be compared. When the study involves comparisons between national groups, these comparisons become meaningful only to the extent that the samples tested do in fact represent the national groups from which they are drawn. When the study involves comparisons of different types of schools within a single national system, it is equally important that the sampling from the different types of schools be representative, so that any differences between them will be accurately representative of the differences that exist in the total group of schools from which the sample was drawn. Insofar as the achievement in single schools is to be compared with that in other single schools, it is important that the students tested in a given school be representative of the totality of students within that school, so that no bias is introduced into the comparison of one school with another. For all of these reasons, the problem of drawing an appropriately representative sample was of very considerable importance for the conduct of the study and for the meaningfulness of the results. Therefore, a good deal of attention was given to the procedures that were set up in each country to sample from the population of schools and of students that were intended to be tested within the country.

At an early stage in the project, each National Center was asked to draw up the plan of sampling for its country. This plan of sampling covered several points. In the first place, it specified certain fractions of the total population that were to be excluded from what will be spoken of later as the "target population" for the country in question. The excluded fraction always included those who because of severe mental disability were not able to profit from the normal program of education and hence were not enrolled in regular schools. Typically the target populations also excluded pupils who were more than a specified number of years retarded in their educational placement, though this aspect of definition of the target population varied from country to country depending upon the policies with respect to retardation that were in operation in the country in question. Excluded from the target population were any members of the age group not in school. These represented very substantial fractions at the grade level from which Population IV was drawn, and also represented fairly substantial fractions at the earlier age levels for those of the developing countries in which universal education is still at best a policy rather than a practice. In some instances, the sample was limited to a geographical region within the country, so that individuals living in other regions were excluded from the target population. For example, the sample in India was limited to the six Hindi-speaking states in which Hindi is the language of instruction.

At the time that the target population was specified, the country also set out a sampling plan. The sampling plan typically specified the bases of stratification of the target population in terms of either region or type of school or both and the basis for selecting schools within strata and students within schools. Estimates were prepared of the total number of students in each stratum so that the number required for the sample could be determined. The objective of the sampling plan was that every student in the target population should have an equal (and, of course, non-zero) chance of appearing in the designed sample for testing. This objective was achieved by adjusting both the size of the sample of students within a school and the number of schools within a given stratum in such a way that the number of pupils to be tested in each stratum bore a constant ratio to the total number of students in the stratum.

Efficiency on the one hand and the need to have an adequately reliable measure of performance within a given school on the other dictated that a sample of moderate size be tested in each school that became a part of the sample for the study. A reasonable size sample per school was considered to be about 30 pupils. The cost of testing more students than this from a given school and analyzing the results would have made it impractical to test an adequate number of schools and consequently to get a sample that efficiently represented the range of schools and of pupils in the country as a whole.

Once the strata had been specified, the usual procedure was to list all of the schools that fell within a given stratum and to draw from that list a random sample of the desired size. In practical reality, in many countries it is impossible to get universal participation by schools that are designated for a sample, so some procedure of replacements was usually required for those schools which declined to participate in the enterprise. This is far from ideal from the sampling point of view, but is hard to avoid in a context of voluntary participation. The use of replacements for a sample does clearly introduce possibilities of bias that are somewhat difficult to estimate, but some amount of such replacement was necessary in at least a fair number of the countries involved in the project.

Within schools, the instructions were set up in such a way that a random sample of students was to be tested. The typical procedure was to test all individuals whose birthdays fell upon randomly selected days of the month. The sampling plan ordinarily called for the designation of specific individuals in each school to constitute the sample tested in that school, this designation being carried out centrally by the National Center rather than locally by the school. A procedure of this type, if followed meticulously, avoids the possibility that the school may exclude from the testing certain individuals whom local officials feel are not favorable representatives of their school's achievement, or may bias in other ways the sample of pupils chosen to be tested.

After the testing had been completed, it was possible to compare the numbers tested within each stratum with the designed number for the sample, to see whether certain strata had been under- or over-sampled. In practice, some degree of under- or over-sampling in certain strata was almost universally the case. The nature of the real world is such that an obtained sample rarely provides a perfect match to the designed sample. Thus, some amount of adjustment for this lack of match between the design and the obtained sample was necessary. This was accomplished by a procedure of weighting. Thus, for example, if the specifications indicated that 100 pupils should have been tested in stratum X, but only 80 pupils were in fact tested who fell within that stratum, the procedure was to consider each of the 80 as representing 1.25 pupils, and to multiply each score by 1.25 in calculating any statistics for the country with respect to pupil characteristics. In most cases, the weighting fell within reasonably narrow limits (roughly 0.5 to 2.0) so that gross adjustments were not required. In a few instances, specific strata within a country were not represented in the obtained sample, and these strata were then designated as part of the excluded population.

It will be noted that Populations I and II were defined as age groups rather than grade groups. This was a very conscious decision, since it was recognized that although age is a uniform attribute from country to country, the meaning of a particular school grade varies as does national policy with respect to holding children back to repeat a school grade. Testing an age group is a much more troublesome enterprise as far as the schools are concerned, since children must be drawn from several grade levels for testing. The degree to which this is true depends upon the frequency and degree of retardation, or possibly acceleration. Countries indicating substantial proportions of the age group not tested either because they were retarded or were not in school at all are listed below, with estimates provided by the country of the percent excluded.

Chile – 33.8% of 10-year-olds more than one year retarded or not attending school,
 – 42.7% of 14-year-olds not attending school.
Hungary – 4–5% of 10-year-olds more than one year retarded and not tested,

– 10–12% of 14-year-olds retarded or not attending school.

India – an unspecified percent of 10-year-olds in grades 1 and 2, and of 14-year-olds in grades 5 and below, and all students in English-speaking private schools.

Israel – 16% of 14-year-olds no longer attending school.

Italy – Population I was defined as 10-year-olds in the 5th grade, excluding approximately 60% of 10-year-olds enrolled in the 4th grade,

– a small proportion of 14-year-olds enrolled in the 7th grade were excluded.

The above instances identify certain instances of discrepancy, one or two of them quite marked. Of course, some children were not in school or were in special schools in all countries, and other minor discrepancies in definition of the target populations and execution of the sampling plan certainly occurred.

TEST ADMINISTRATION

Any large scale cross-national survey is a very complex enterprise involving careful coordination at a number of levels. Coordination is required at the international level to make sure that the procedures in each country are carried out in the same way, that the materials are uniform from country to country, and that the supervision of local units is adequately provided for. Coordination at the national level is essential if the testing and data collection are to be carried out in a uniform way in each of the participating communities or schools. Coordination at the local level is essential when information is being gathered from a number of teachers and when several test administrators may be participating in the conduct of the testing. This section describes in general outline the procedures that were carried out to coordinate activities and to guarantee, as far as possible, uniform procedures for the collection of data in each country, each school, and each class or group that was tested.

International coordination was concerned primarily with guidance of the activities of the National Centers. This included the preparation of materials and directions that were made available to the National Centers for their use in coordinating the work within their own country. It also included detailed briefing of a National Technical Officer, responsible for the conduct of testing in his country, at a week-long meeting at which all materials and procedures were reviewed. First and foremost among the materials that were prepared at IEA International, the headquarters of the project, growing out of work of the subject matter committees, were the actual tests themselves. After these committees had examined the data from preliminary try-outs and assembled the items in the desired sequence, the tests were reproduced centrally together with the directions for the examinee and for the administrator of the tests. The tests, together with directions, were then distributed to each of the National Centers. All test materials were initially developed in English, and each National Center had the responsibility for translating materials from English into the language of the country.

At the same time that the tests were distributed, copies of the several questionnaires developed by the questionnaire committee for the students, teachers, and school administrators were also reproduced centrally and distributed to each of the participating countries. Where a country had problems with translation, these were ordinarily discussed with IEA International so that the phrasing of the questionnaires could be as comparable as possible from one language to another.

In addition to the tests and the questionnaires, manuals of procedure were developed centrally. These included manuals for procedures at each of three levels. In the first place, there was a manual of procedures for the National Center itself, spelling out step by step in considerable detail the activities that the National Center was to carry out in order that the appropriate data could be received back for analysis as efficiently as possible. At a second level, a manual of procedures was prepared to be distributed to the test coordinator at the local level. This was again quite detailed, giving in sequence each activity that the local coordinator was expected to carry out, telling him just how each of the types of material that he would receive was to be distributed and indicating just what information was to be obtained from whom. At the third level, manuals of directions were prepared for the individuals who would actually administer the tests, giving them essentially verbatim instructions as to what they were to say and how the actual testing itself was to be carried out.

One reason why full and detailed directions were needed was that in most countries the tests and questionnaire responses were recorded on Measurement Research Center mark-sensed cards so that they could be processed in a highly automated fashion by the Measurement Research Center in Iowa City in the United States. The cards provide answer spaces in which precoded responses may be marked with ordinary pencil and then transcribed to magnetic tape by optical scanner. The data cards from the test administration were assembled by the National Center, checked for proper marking and cleaned up where necessary, and shipped to Iowa City, where they were processed. All the items of information that were included on the several data cards were recorded on magnetic tape and these tapes provided the raw material for further analyses. It was, therefore, important that the procedures for filling out the cards be meticulously followed in each participating school and it was to guarantee this, as far as was humanly possible, that the various sets of very complete directions were provided.

The National Centers had several important responsibilities in the coordination of the testing enterprise. The first of these was to translate all the tests, questionnaires and manuals into the language of the country so that the testing could be carried out in the vernacular. A second was to reproduce all materials in sufficient quantities to provide for testing at the local levels. Data cards were produced centrally and supplied to National Centers. Thirdly, the National Center had the responsibility of distributing the materials to the local centers. In many countries, all the materials for a single examinee were packaged in a single envelope. These sets, together with Teacher and School Questionnaires and instructional manuals comprised the shipment to a local center. The National Center had the further responsibility of gathering together the tests and questionnaires from the schools as the testing was completed, checking to see that the materials from the school were complete and correctly filled out, and forwarding the material to the Measurement Research Center for processing. Some of the data that could not be precoded had to be coded at the National Center and entered on the data cards for further processing. In addition, all School Questionnaires were coded and put on punch cards at the National Center.

A further responsibility of the National Center was to fill out the so-called National Case Study Questionnaire. In this document a rather extended series of questions was raised about the policies and procedures of the national educational system. These dealt with such matters as the proportion of individuals at different ages who were actually in school, the national policy with respect to the age of beginning school, the pattern of types of schools at different age levels, and many other inquiries about the educational system and the economic development of the country involved. This questionnaire material was gathered in order to provide some kind of background for interpreting national differences in educational achievement, and seeing what some of the correlates of national achievement were.

In some countries at least, the National Center undertook to provide training sessions for the local coordinators and test administrators. This was true especially in countries in which objective types of tests were unfamiliar and in which the teachers would have been likely to have had no previous experience in administering this type of instrument. Groups of examiners were brought together and briefed with respect to the conduct of testing and the precautions to be observed in such a testing enterprise.

Responsibility for the actual conduct of testing rested largely at the local level. Testing was carried out in as many as two or three hundred localities in a given country, and so it was manifestly impossible to provide centralized administration of the actual tests themselves. A local coordinator was designated who was responsible for the local arrangements and for local supervision. The local coordinator received the test materials from the National Center, distributed them as needed in his own school or school system, provided training as needed at the local level for the persons who would be administering the tests, and gathered up the data cards and testing materials when the testing was completed so that the materials could be sent back to the National Center. At an earlier stage, the local coordinator also carried some responsibility for sending the National Center the information on the basis of which the local sampling was carried out and the students were chosen who were actually to be tested in the testing enterprise.

As would inevitably be true of such a highly dispersed undertaking, there were instances in which something went wrong at the local level. Ordinarily the National Center could maintain contact with the local unit and could remedy the deficiency or collect the information that was missing if the materials were carefully checked as soon as they were received from the local test unit. However, it is true that not all items of information were gathered in all localities. In particular some of the items of information on School and Teacher Questionnaires were missing or uninterpretable. The responses sometimes took values that were inconsistent with what was reasonable or possible for the particular datum involved. These impossible values were treated as missing data and served to increase the number of missing items in the data. When correlations were calculated between variables, they were based upon only those schools or individuals for which both items of information were available.

In spite of occasional lapses, the testing was generally successfully carried out. In the case of Reading Comprehension, results were obtained from 15 countries involving a total of 1 670 schools and 34 344 students in Population I, 1 752 schools and 39 307 students in Population II, and 1 209 schools and 29 474 students in Population IV. The data from these schools and students, together with a sampling of the teachers in each school constitute the raw material upon which the analyses reported in the following chapters are based.

Chapter 4

Psychometric Properties of the Instruments

Before turning to an examination of the factors associated with reading performance in the several countries, it is appropriate to examine the psychometric properties of the tests that were used in the study. Did they have adequate reliability not only in English but also in the several languages into which they were translated? Were the subscores for different reading skills meaningfully distinct, so that there is some justification for further study of the subscores? How much overlap is there between the measure of reading comprehension and the measure of reading speed? Between each of these and the measure of word knowledge? Are these relationships relatively uniform from country to country, and from language to language, or are they quite variable?

RELIABILITY OF TESTS

Reliability data are reported below for total test scores and for subtest scores. In the case of all the tests except reading speed, internal consistency estimates of reliability are reported. For reading speed, and also for reading comprehension total score, data are provided based on separately timed alternate forms of the test.

Reading Comprehension Total Score

Reliability coefficients for reading comprehension total score are presented in Table 4.1. This table displays two estimates of reliability for each country and level. The estimate in the first column at each age level was derived by Kuder–Richardson Formula 20 (Kuder and Richardson, 1937), and is based on the internal consistency of all the items in the test. The estimate in the second column is based on the correlation between two subtests that were separately timed and designed to be equivalent in difficulty and nature. The correlation shown has been corrected by the Spearman–Brown Prophecy Formula

Table 4.1. *Reliability of Reading Comprehension. Total Score*

Country	10-year-olds		14-year-olds		End of secondary	
	KR-20	Alternate form	KR-20	Alternate form	KR-20	Alternate form
Belgium (Fl)	.824	.797	.828	.748	.792	.757
Belgium (Fr)	.836	.802	.798	.772	.795	.733
Chile	.834	.778	.854	.838	.774	.690
England	.890	.872	.887	.864	.819	.742
Finland	.879	.855	.862	.837	.738	.654
Hungary	.844	.798	.826	.800	.778	.746
India	.835	.753	.684	.664	.523	.463
Iran	.736	.676	.640	.557	.626	.491
Israel	.888	.871	.898	.886	.852	—
Italy	.856	.812	.819	.799	.834	.796
Netherlands	.837	.796	.843	.801	.721	.646
New Zealand	—	—	.875	.857	.779	.714
Scotland	.878	.863	.881	.868	.777	.747
Sweden	.877	.851	.865	.834	.808	.751
United States	.888	.867	.885	.851	.873	.859
Median	.850	.807	.854	.834	.779	.740

(see Stanley, 1971) to yield an estimate of reliability for the total test.

The values in Table 4.1 indicate that the tests were providing a reasonably precise estimate of reading performance in most countries and at most levels. Coefficients falling between 0.75 and 0.85 are typical. As might be expected, the KR-20 estimates are uniformly higher than those based on alternate forms. The alternate-forms coefficients reflect variations in rate of work for the appreciable number of students who did not complete all the items, and variations due to the fact that the two forms are based on entirely different passages. Probably more attention should be paid to the alternate-forms coefficients as representing a sound, conservative estimate of the precision of the tests.

One can see a slight tendency for the reliabilities to be higher in English-speaking countries. This is not surprising, since the basic developmental and editorial work on the items was done on the English language version. All passages and items were tried out in one or two languages in addition to English, but not in all of the languages used in the study. It is quite possible that some clarity was lost in translation either of the passages or the test items or both. However, with one or two exceptions that are discussed more fully below, the losses in precision are slight. The tests functioned relatively satisfactorily in translation.

There was a general tendency for reliabilities to be lower for the group tested at the end of the secondary school. The only exception to this trend was in the United States. Lowered reliability seems almost certainly a function of the reduced range of talent in the terminal group. Except in the United States, the poor readers have been largely eliminated by this time. Variability has been reduced, and as a result the correlation coefficients are lower. It is also probably true that the problems of translation were most acute for the difficult materials in the Population IV level test.

In India and Iran, the reliabilities of the tests were disappointingly low. There are several factors that might have contributed to this result, but one major factor appears to have been that the tests were too difficult for students in these countries. Thus, an examination of item statistics shows the following numbers of test items in which the percent of correct answers did not fall above a chance level (25% correct on four-choice items):

	India	Iran
Population I	8	19
Population II	17	12
Population IV	24	23

Thus, from 20 to 40% of the items were apparently almost non-functioning in these countries. It is possible, of course, that item difficulty stemmed in part from difficulties in translation, rather than from basic deficiencies in literacy of the students. Lack of familiarity with multiple-choice tests may also have contributed to poor, and consequently erratic performance. Finally, it is true that most of the passages were contributed by European countries or the United States, and they may have presented more difficulty to students from a non-European background.

Reading Comprehension Subscores

A number of subscores were derived from the Reading Comprehension test. These were of two types. One subscore was for items common to two successive levels of the test. Those "anchor" items were designed to permit an estimate of the increment in comprehension level from age 10 to 14 and from age 14 to the end of secondary school. Other subscores represented groups of items that were judged to deal with a particular type of reading process. The following five subscores were recorded, based on categories originally suggested by F. B. Davis (1944):

A. Ability to determine the meaning of a word or phrase in context (used only at 10-year-old level),

B. Ability to follow the organization of a passage and to identify antecedents and references in it (used only at 14-year-old and end-of-secondary-school levels),

C. Ability to answer questions that are specifically answered in the passage,

D. Ability to draw inferences from a passage about its contents, and

E. Ability to determine the writer's purpose, intent and point of view.

Since these subscores were in many instances based on only a few items, the reliabilities were naturally relatively low. Information about reliability of the subscores is important in any further comparisons to estimate their degree of overlapping. Evidence on the reliability of the anchor tests is needed to permit an estimate of the overlapping of the successive groups in true score for reading ability. Reliability analyses were carried out for a subset of nine countries for which test data were available at a relatively early date, and these are shown in Table 4.2.

Word Knowledge Test

Reliability coefficients for the word knowledge test are shown in Table 4.3. This test was also designed with overlap between successive levels, so that some estimate might be made of increments in word knowledge from age 10 to age 14 and from age 14 to the end of secondary education. Reliability coefficients are shown for the total test of 40 items as well as for the shorter anchor tests.

The median of the reliability coefficients for this test was approximately 0.86 in Population I, 0.81 in Population II and 0.76 in Population IV. For the investment of ten minutes of testing time, it appears to have yielded a reasonable amount of information on each individual's basic store of word meanings. As discussed elsewhere, this test did not appear to be as uniform from language to language in the task that it presented to examinees as did the test based on reading connected and meaningful prose.

Reading Speed Test

Because of its highly speeded character, the only way in which a meaningful estimate of reliability could be obtained for the reading speed test was to give two separately timed tests to groups of examinees, and obtain the correlation between the two forms. Fortunately, a second form was available. This had been developed to serve as practice test in the regular administration. Using this as an

Table 4.2. *Reliability Coefficients for Reading Comprehension Test Subscores*

	Anchor I to II	Item type			
		A	C	D	E
A. *Population I: 10-year-olds*					
No. of items	7	3	13	18	5
Chile	.319	.056	.761	.548	.229
England	.488	.235	.814	.699	.290
Finland	.441	.168	.791	.663	.448
Hungary	.420	.145	.740	.566	.278
Netherlands	.422	.169	.728	.611	.132
Scotland	.449	.239	.806	.669	.266
Sweden	.428	.123	.793	.706	.316
United States	.545	.289	.787	.707	.355
Median	.434	.168	.789	.666	.284

Table 4.2. (*Cont.*)

	Anchor I to II	Anchor II to IV	Item type			
			B	C	D	E
B. *Population II: 14-year-olds*						
No. of items	7	13	4	7	25	6
Chile	.490	.574	.224	.649	.753	.263
England	.503	.638	.264	.612	.823	.299
Finland	.509	.669	.451	.579	.762	.263
Hungary	.367	.604	.453	.545	.681	.281
Netherlands	.413	.657	.309	.538	.707	.310
New Zealand	.521	.670	.358	.570	.802	.282
Scotland	.527	.640	.257	.589	.817	.246
Sweden	.484	.589	.283	.585	.769	.438
United States	.575	.684	.350	.560	.808	.414
Median	.503	.640	.309	.579	.769	.282

Table 4.2. (*Cont.*)

	Anchor II to IV	Item type			
		B	C	D	E
C. *Population IV: End of secondary*					
No. of items	13	6	9	17	6
Chile	.586	.256	.457	.568	.119
England	.488	.273	.461	.649	.226
Finland	.416	.253	.332	.546	.209
Hungary	.500	.303	.448	.560	.177
Netherlands	.441	.088	.221	.582	.057
New Zealand	.432	.177	.463	.594	.142
Scotland	.406	.172	.373	.610	.112
Sweden	.553	.268	.404	.623	.188
United States	.672	.317	.650	.679	.393
Median	.458	.256	.448	.594	.177

Table 4.3. *Reliability Coefficients for Word Knowledge Test*

	Total test			Anchor items			
				Population I to Population II		Population II to Population IV	
	Population I	Population II	Population IV	Population I	Population II	Population II	Population IV
No. of items	40	40	40	13	13	21	21
Belgium (Fl)	.763	.793	.730	*	*	*	*
Belgium (Fr)	.818	.838	.802	*	*	*	*
Chile	.904	.850	.842	.719	.710	.718	.736
England	.874	.833	.765	.671	.694	.704	.634
Finland	.775	.725	.676	.313	.487	.580	.554
Hungary	.881	.860	.758	.705	.697	.731	.614
India	.890	.812	.779	*	*	*	*
Iran	.870	.799	.747	*	*	*	*
Israel	.848	.845	.792	*	*	*	*
Italy	.873	.824	.770	*	*	*	*
Netherlands	.763	.750	.681	.515	.548	.559	.563
New Zealand	*	.816	.787	*	.674	.690	.674
Scotland	.865	.804	.753	.639	.672	.661	.636
Sweden	.709	.672	.742	.389	.546	.413	.621
United States	.815	.741	.759	.548	.593	.586	.652

* Analysis not available.

Table 4.4. *Alternate Forms Reliability Coefficients of Reading Speed Test*

	Population I		Population II	
	Attempted	Correct	Attempted	Correct
Hungary	.87	.85	.89	.87
New Zealand	—	—	.66	.64
United States	.64	.75	.82	.80

alternate form, special studies on reliability were carried out in Hungary, New Zealand and the United States. The alternate-forms reliabilities for number attempted and number correct are shown in Table 4.4.

The evidence on reliability is somewhat inconsistent from group to group, for reasons that are not entirely clear. However, as a rough approximation, it appears that the reliability of the four-minute reading speed sample is of the order of 0.7 or 0.8—high enough to permit useful studies of individual and group correlates of the score.

CORRELATIONS OF READING COMPREHENSION SUBSCORES

In part as a basis for judging whether it would be fruitful to carry out detailed analyses of the external correlates of the reading comprehension subscores, correlations among the subscores were computed for each population and each country. The raw correlation coefficients are difficult to interpret because of the often low and rather widely varied reliabilities of the subscores. Correlations were therefore corrected for attenuation using the reliability coefficients from Table 4.2. Because the data would be quite voluminous and not very meaningful, tables are not shown for each separate country. Table 4.5 shows the median corrected correlation and the range of values obtained for different countries for each pair of subtests in each population.

Clearly, the corrected correlations of the reading subtest scores are very high. Due to (1) sampling errors in reliabilities and correlation coefficients, and (2) a sharing of common content in that items of different categories are based upon a common passage, the corrected correlations frequently come out to be greater than 1.00. In a few instances, especially in Population I, even the median correlation

Table 4.5. *Median and Range of Corrected Correlations Between Reading Comprehension Subtests*

	Subtest C		Subtest D		Subtest E	
	Median	Range	Median	Range	Median	Range
Population I						
Subtest A	.89	.76–1.09	1.03	.96–1.13	1.25	1.13–1.65
Subtest C			.99	.96–1.02	.94	.89–1.00
Subtest D					1.03	.93–1.09
Population II						
Subtest B	.76	.69–.80	.78	.70–.87	.79	.58–.98
Subtest C			1.00	.96–1.05	.96	.80–1.06
Subtest D					.96	.92–1.06
Population IV						
Subtest B	.86	.79–1.00	.86	.76–.97	.88	.73–1.03
Subtest C			.94	.91–.97	.84	.72–1.09
Subtest D					.81	.70–.94

takes on such a logically meaningless value. Certainly, there is no support for any separate analysis of the subtests in Population I or II. Even in Population IV the corrected correlations are high enough to indicate that any attempt to distinguish between them will result in very fragile results. Little further attention will therefore be paid to the subtest scores.

Correlation of Reading Speed and Comprehension

It is of some interest to inquire to what extent speed of reading quite simple material is a skill distinct from comprehension of text of greater difficulty given with fairly liberal time limits. The raw correlations between the speed and comprehension measures are shown in Table 4.6. Unfortunately, data on the reliability of the speed test are limited to modest supplementary studies in Hungary, New Zealand and the United States, so that no country-by-country correction for attenuation is possible in the case of the correlations of Table 4.6, and it is impossible to tell whether differences in the correlations from one country to another are due to differences in the reliability of the measures or to differences in overlapping of the two functions measured.

The median uncorrected correlation between reading speed score

Table 4.6. *Correlations of Number Attempted on Reading Speed Test with Reading Comprehension Score*

Country	Population I	Population II
Belgium (Fl)	.362	.342
Belgium (Fr)	.323	.252
Chile	.290	.275
England	.468	.469
Finland	.365	.466
Hungary	.334	.377
India	.139	.073
Iran	− .031	.141
Israel	.318	.396
Italy	.083	.279
Netherlands	.332	.277
New Zealand	—	.495
Scotland	.481	.500
Sweden	.369	.400
United States	.311	.552

and reading comprehension score is 0.33 in Population I and 0.38 in Population II. Using 0.81 and 0.83 as estimates of the reliability of the comprehension test in the two populations and 0.75 and 0.80 as estimates for the speed test, one obtains median corrected correlations of 0.42 and 0.47 as estimates of the correlation between error-free measures of the two functions. From country to country, the correlations are fairly closely similar, except for India and Iran in both populations and Italy for Population I. In these five instances, the correlations are close to zero. In view of the generally low scores —and the substantial number of chance scores—in India and Iran, one is inclined to feel that a number of the poorer readers simply dashed through the reading speed test, marking pretty much at random and not really reading the passages, and that those who really attempted to read the passages were correspondingly delayed. Except for these instances, there was a general tendency for those who could read more difficult material with understanding to read the simpler material rapidly.

Correlation of Word Knowledge with Reading
Comprehension and Speed

It has always been clear that ability to read with understanding depends upon knowledge of the meanings of the words in which a

Table 4.7. *Correlations of Word Knowledge with Reading Measures*

| Country | Reading Comprehension | | | Reading Speed | |
	Population I	Population II	Population IV	Population I	Population II
Belgium (Fl)	.537	.591	.500	.317	.281
Belgium (Fr)	.588	.619	.481	.162	.225
Chile	.543	.508	.577	.292	.244
England	.735	.698	.497	.423	.416
Finland	.617	.654	.395	.272	.431
Hungary	.594	.533	.389	.236	.307
India	.569	.387	.320	.148	.084
Iran	.498	.427	.294	−.110	.131
Israel	.651	.674	—	.253	.365
Italy	.580	.587	.446	.055	.320
Netherlands	.620	.624	.310	.265	.250
New Zealand	—	.685	.536	—	.483
Scotland	.716	.719	.579	.440	.473
Sweden	.559	.598	.584	.289	.304
United States	.735	.693	.679	.341	.463

message is expressed. However, it seems worth exploring how completely reading performance is determined by word knowledge at different levels and in different countries. Given the data, it also seems instructive to examine the overlap between word knowledge and speed of reading simple material. Correlations are presented in Table 4.7. In the case of reading comprehension, reliability data are available making it possible to show correlations corrected for attenuation as well as the raw correlations.

The median obtained correlation between word knowledge and reading comprehension, taken across countries, is 0.59 for Population I, 0.62 for Population II and 0.49 for Population IV. Correlations run as low as 0.31 and as high as 0.74. The lower correlations arise in part because of lower reliabilities of the tests correlated. However, even when corrected for unreliability, the correlations vary quite substantially. The median corrected correlations are 0.71 in Population I, 0.75 in Population II, and 0.66 in Population IV. However, corrected values go as low as 0.48 (Iran, Population IV), and as high as 0.86 (Scotland, Population II).

There is a tendency, even after correction for unreliability, for correlations to be highest in English-speaking countries. The results provide a suggestion that the large total vocabulary and wide range of near synonyms in English make size of vocabulary a more crucial component for reading of English than for reading of some other sparser languages.

Correlations of word knowledge with reading speed are generally quite modest, running slightly lower than the correlations between speed and comprehension.

REFERENCES

Davis, F. B. "Fundamental Factors of Comprehension in Reading." *Psychometrika* 9, 1944, pp. 185–197.

Kuder, G. F. and Richardson, M. W. "The Theory of the Estimation of Test Reliability." *Psychometrika* 2, 1937, pp. 151–160.

Stanley, J. C. Section on the Spearman-Brown Prophecy Formula in "Reliability". In R. L. Thorndike (Ed.), *Educational Measurement.* Washington, D.C.: American Council on Education, 1971, pp. 394–396.

Chapter 5

Procedures for Analyzing Correlates of Reading Achievement

The technical and methodological aspects of data analysis for the cycle of cross-national studies of educational achievement of which this study of reading is one are described in full detail in Volume VIII of the series of reports of the program. However, some explication of the problems and the procedures is needed here if the following chapters are to be read with understanding. The presentation that follows will be somewhat sketchy, is intended to be relatively non-technical, and may not be mathematically precise in some respects. It is designed to give the person who is not a statistical specialist a general grasp of the problems and procedures.

The basic question to which we address ourselves is: What accounts for differences in ability to read? We consider differences at three levels: (1) differences among individuals in each country without regard to the particular school in which they are found, (2) differences among schools within the same country in average performance, and (3) differences among countries in overall average achievement. In order to answer the questions, information has been sought about a wide range of items concerning the individual's home, his family, his interests and attitudes; concerning his school and its resources; concerning his community; and concerning his country and its national educational system. These items have been gathered not blindly, but in terms of either expressed or implicit hypotheses about the determiners of reading achievement or of achievement in Science or Literature which were studied at the same time.

A hypothesis is ordinarily expressed in fairly general terms, such as: Reading achievement is positively related to amount and variety of reading material available in the home. However, it has typically been necessary to rely upon rather indirect and rather incomplete *indicators* in attempting to test such an hypothesis. Thus, to provide indicators of availability of reading material in the home each student was asked the following questions:

1. About how many books are there in your home?
2. How often is a dictionary used by anyone in your home?
3. Does your family receive or do you regularly read a *daily* newspaper?
4. About how many different magazines does your family receive each month?

Practical considerations made it necessary to rely almost entirely on questionnaires as a source of information. Since the responses to these questions may not be fully accurate, and since they cover only some aspects and not all of the possible facts representing such a construct as "supply of reading matter in the home," the available data must be considered only *partial indicators* rather than *complete measures* of the variables with which this study is basically concerned.

Information about individual pupils was obtained from a questionnaire that the pupil filled out, information about teachers and the school from questionnaires filled out by teachers and by an administrative officer in each school, and information about the national culture and educational pattern from a questionnaire filled out by each IEA National Center.

Collectively, the questionnaires provided a large number of bits of specific information. It would have been possible to examine the relationship to reading score of each bit of information about, for example, the individual pupil. However, this would have been unsatisfactory for at least three reasons:

1. The single specific item might tap only a very small segment of the background factor in which one is interested,

2. With such a large number of predictor variables, occasional chance fluctuations might produce values of correlations that would distort the basic pattern of underlying relationships, and

3. The basic logic underlying inclusion of related sets of items would be lost.

For these reasons, the initial analyses of the data were devoted to combining certain of the single indicators into a smaller number of composites, which could then be studied as predictors of achievement, and to identifying a reduced set of variables that gave consistent indication that they might be related to achievement.

Combination of indicators into composites was done partly on rational bases and partly on empirical ones. On an a priori basis, the indicator variables were first subdivided into major groupings. In the case of the between-schools analyses, for example, major groupings were:

1. Out-of-school variables, primarily home and family variables,
2. Type of school or program,
3. School curricular and instructional variables, including characteristics of the instruction and of the teachers, and
4. "Kindred" variables, representing current characteristics of the students in the school.

Within each major grouping certain of the variables appeared to go together in logical clusters. One illustration is the four indicators of availability of reading resources. A second would be the combination of Father's education, Mother's education and Father's occupational level into a single index of socioeconomic status of the home. Weights for combining sets of indicators such as these into a single composite index were generally determined empirically by pooling the correlational data from a number of countries and then determining the weighting that would, on the average, best predict the reading test score.

Two major types of analysis were then undertaken. In one the investigators selected a priori from the complete set of indicators those for which there appeared to be some rationale indicating that they ought to be related to reading achievement. These were examined singly, and sometimes in combination, to see to what extent they did in fact relate to reading achievement. The relationships were examined either as calculated (i.e., zero-order correlations) or with one or more input factors partialled out. Measures of input included socioeconomic status of the family and type of school program to which the student was assigned.

In this type of a priori analysis, the 14 or 15 participating countries were thought of as replications of an investigation, and attention was focussed primarily upon relationships that appeared consistently in all or almost all of the countries within the study. Where a relationship varies from country to country, with correlations often almost evenly balanced between positive and negative, it is of course *possible* that the indicator truly has variable and even opposite significance from one country to another. However, when the correlations are quite small, as they typically were in this research, a simpler and perhaps more plausible explanation is that the variations represent only chance fluctuations around a near zero "true" value. It has seemed better to ignore such small and erratic relationships, rather than to seek for devious explanations of them.

A second type of analysis proceeded at once more systematically and more empirically by a type of step-wise regression analysis in which blocks of variables, and selected variables within the block were systematically added to a prediction equation and the contribution of each to the specification of level of reading ability was determined. The steps in this procedure will be set forth in some detail at this point.

When the test and questionnaire data had been gathered from students, teachers and school administrators, coded, and organized as a data file on magnetic tape, there existed a couple of hundred bits of information on each individual student and several hundred bits characterizing each school. For the student, some items on the tape represented responses to single specific questions, e.g., "Are you a boy or a girl?" Others represented scores derived from a fairly extended set of questions, for example, a reading comprehension score or a score expressing degree of liking for school. For the school, many items represented averages or percentages based on student scores of the types just described, others were averages or percentages based on the responses of several teachers in the school, while still others were single responses recorded by an administrator as characterizing the school as a whole.

Especially in the case of the school data, the number of variables was unmanageably large, in view of the number of schools for which data had been obtained. Depending upon the country and the age group, number of schools ranged from as low as approximately 30 to as high as about 250. With samples of this size, it becomes logically absurd to analyze a battery of several hundred predictors. It was necessary in some way to screen out from the mass of data the variables that showed real promise of functioning as contributing predictors.

Preliminary scrutiny of the data made it abundantly clear that to a considerable extent the output of a school in terms of average reading score depended upon the input in terms of home background and prior academic level of the students. A simple indicator of home background was the father's level of occupation (scaled so as to maximize the correlation between the scaling and reading score), and some indication of prior progress was the type of school program in which the student had been placed. When deciding which school variables offered promise as predictors of achievement it seemed important to hold these input factors constant through methods of partial correlation. This was done, and the residual correlation of each variable with the reading score was obtained for each country. The residual correlations were plotted on a scale from $+1.00$ to -1.00, so that it was fairly easy to spot any variable that showed residual correlations differing appreciably from zero in most countries or of substantial size in at least a few countries.

Many variables were eliminated from the regression analysis at this point because they showed little or no consistent relationship to the reading score. Those that showed some promise empirically or that were of special a priori interest were retained and analyzed in a second more rigorous partial correlation study. In this analysis a "School Handicap Score" was created for each country by weighting in combination for all ages:

1. Father's occupation,
2. Number of books in the home,
3. Use of dictionary in the home, and
4. Numbers of siblings (reversed),

and in Population II (14-year-olds) and Population IV (end of secondary education) also:

5. Father's education, and
6. Mother's education.

The variables were combined with a weight that would maximize the correlation of the composite with the reading test score. Of course for the analysis when the school was the unit, the variables going into the composite were averages based on all the pupils from that school.

On the basis of this second set of partial correlations, a further screening was made to weed out variables that now added nothing to the prediction of the reading score beyond what was possible on the basis of this input variable alone. The numbers of variables retained for the final regression analysis were as follows:

	Between students	Between schools
Population I	31	36
Population II	34	31
Population IV	32	32

The regression analysis was carried out in stages, adding blocks of variables in the following order:

1. The School Handicap Score, determined as described above and representing the character of student input, and in addition the variables Age of student and Sex of student,

2. Type of school and Type of program,

3. School variables relating to school organization, characteristics of teachers, or instructional procedures, and the like,

4. Kindred variables, consisting of present characteristics of students—their activities, interests, or attitudes—that seem more appropriately considered concomitants than causes of reading ability, and

5. Word knowledge test score, as a type of index of the general ability level of the student.

The rationale for entering blocks of variables in this order is one of chronology of impact upon the student. The home variables are prior to and outside the control of the school, and determine what type of an input the school has available to it to work with. Type of school or program to which a student is admitted (to the extent that these are significant predictors) is an index of success on *prior* steps of the academic ladder, and is also indicative of quality of input. School variables have their effect upon this input; the kindred variables describe a number of other characteristics of the individual as he *now* is that result from the complex of earlier home and school influences and that to some extent enrich the present description of the good reader. Word knowledge provides a supplementary index of current ability level.

In the chapters that follow, the factors associated with reading achievement will first be analyzed in relation to the achievement of individual students, focusing on the factors that may vary even for students within a specific school. Attention will next be directed at the "input" and "treatment" factors that are related to between-school differences in reading performance. In each of these analyses, the several countries may be considered replications of the investigation, and we shall be interested in the degree to which the effective factors and their relative weights remain the same from country to country. Where the pattern of prediction is radically different in one country from the pattern in others, an attempt will be made to seek plausible reasons for the difference.

Comparison of level of performance in different countries represents a rather minor component of the analysis of results from the present study. The 15 countries studied differ in so many ways with respect to language, culture, level of economic development, and pattern of education that it is an almost hopeless task to try to isolate critical factors accounting for differences in achievement. It will be possible to see rather gross differences between the economically developed countries and three less-developed countries, with the result that almost any index of educational or economic development shows a substantial correlation with reading score. Some correlations of such factors with reading achievement will be shown.

The amount and source of variation *within* a country is also of some interest. To what extent are the pupils within a given school uniform in their ability, so that much of the variation occurs between schools? Conversely, to what extent are schools uniform, so that most of the variation is of students within a school? Analysis of the within-school as compared to the between-school variability will be carried out in order to throw some light on this point.

As different countries are compared, it will be of interest to examine not only the score at each age level taken separately, but also the increment in reading ability from one age to the next. An estimate of this increment will be derived from the common "anchor" items that appear in the test for both Populations I and II and for both Populations II and IV. Because these tests are short and consequently rather unreliable, it will be important to use estimated true scores as a basis for establishing equivalent scores on the complete tests at levels I and II and levels II and IV. The technical details of this procedure are set forth more fully in Chapter 8.

In addition to the analyses of the reading and word knowledge tests as composite measures, information was obtained for each population and each country on the difficulty and discrimination indices of each test item, and on the popularity of the several distractors (error choices) for each item. An examination of these made it possible to evaluate the extent to which the specific test tasks retained their characteristics through translation and use in different national cultures. These findings are described in Chapter 9.

Chapter 6

Factors Associated with Individual Student Differences in Reading Achievement

In this chapter, attention is focussed on the factors in the background and characteristics of the individual student that are associated with his level of reading ability. Attention is directed primarily at those attributes which lie outside the school setting. Specific school factors, which are in general uniform for all the individuals in a school, are considered in Chapter 7. In the present analyses, all of the individuals for a given population in a given country have been pooled. Thus, differences arise in part because students within a single school vary; they arise in part because the students in one school differ from the students in another school. However, the components that are studied in this chapter are largely characteristics of the individual rather than of the school environment in which he is embedded. The questions asked are of the type: If a student has parents who are more (or less) interested in his school progress than the average of children of his educational level, does he tend to read better (or worse) than the average student in his group?

THE COMBINING OF VARIABLES

A number of items of information were gathered about each individual. Some of these can appropriately be grouped, primarily on logical and rational grounds, into clusters to which a common designation can be given. Attention will be paid here to three such clusters in particular. One may be called the socioeconomic level of the home, one may be called the resources in the home for reading stimulation, and one may be called level of parental interest and involvement in schooling. In addition to these composites, there are a number of single variables that may be examined as possible predictors of reading achievement. In what follows, first a description will be given of the manner in which the composite scores were generated, and then an examination made of the relationships of the composites and of individual variables to the criterion measures of Reading Comprehension.

In addition to variables that can be thought of as part of the student's background in terms of which the student approaches the problems of education, information was obtained on a number of other variables that may be thought of as current characteristics of the student. These are more appropriately thought of as current correlates of reading achievement than as predictors or prior determinants. Examples of this type of variable are those dealing with the student's report of his amount and type of free reading, amount of homework and the type of school program in which he is enrolled. These have been called "kindred" variables serving to describe a good reader as he currently exists rather than as background for the development of his present reading skills. They will be analyzed as a separate group.

The first composite variable dealt with was one that would describe the socioeconomic level of the home in fairly concrete and objective terms. For this, in Populations II and IV, the student's report on three characteristics of his family was available as follows: (1) a report of his father's occupation, (2) a report of his father's education, (3) a report of his mother's education. In Population I, only the report of father's occupation was available. The variable Father's occupation was coded within each country into anywhere from 7 to 9 occupational categories representing main classes in an occupational hierarchy. It was intended that the occupations be arranged in ascending or hierarchical order in terms of general level of status and economic return within the total occupational structure of the country. Each country was allowed a certain amount of leeway in defining the categories, because it was recognized that the perception of occupational groups may not be identical from one country to another. Thus, in the United States the categories were described as follows:

Code Number	Category
9	Professional, technical and kindred workers
8	Managers, officials and proprietors, including farm owners and managers
7	White collar workers
6	Skilled manual workers
5	Semi-skilled manual workers

4	Farm workers, fishery, forestry and kindred groups
3	Domestic and personal service workers
2	Laborers
1	Unclassifiable
0	Unknown

In each country, coding was done centrally on the basis of the student's report of the specific job that his father held.

In order to translate the coding of Father's occupation into a score that would be an effective predictor of reading achievement, a regression analysis was carried out of the several categories of the score, assigning each individual a code of 1 for the category in which his father's occupation fell and a code of zero for all the other ocupations. So, in the United States, the nine categories of occupation were treated as nine dummy variables, and that weighting was determined for this set of nine variables that would maximize the correlation of the set with Reading Comprehension score. Thus, Father's occupation was empirically scaled in such a way as to maximize its predictive effectiveness. The scaling was different from country to country. In a number of countries, the categories as originally defined were found not to have been in order from low to high, in terms of student reading test score. Thus, in Finland, the students in Category 5 were found to show a higher level of reading achievement than the students in Categories 6 and 8 which were above it in rank on the occupational scale. Thus, to treat the original categories as an ordered scale would not always have been appropriate. The empirical scaling rectified this situation whenever it occurred.

Scaling of Father's occupation was carried out for Population II, 14-year-olds, and these scale values were applied in Populations I and IV. It was believed that this would provide the most appropriate scaling because, on the one hand, the 14-year-olds would be mature enough to provide reasonably accurate information on their father's occupation while, on the other hand, the sample of 14-year-olds would be representative of the full spectrum of occupational levels and pupil ability. It was feared that the questionnaire responses of 10-year-olds might be less dependable. For the end-of-secondary group, selectivity would have operated to such an extent that many of the children from parents in lower occupational categories, and especially the less able students, would have been eliminated and the underlying relationship would have been distorted.

In the original data analysis, correlations were reported between each of the seven to nine dummy variables and each of the other measures that were gathered on the individuals in the sample. Subsequently, the regression weights established for each category of the occupational system were applied, and the correlation of the composite variable, Father's occupation, with each of the remaining variables was determined. That is, the nine separate variables were reduced to one composite variable in which the weights represented the weights to maximize the prediction of reading achievement, and this variable was correlated with the remaining variables. In Populations II and IV, the composite variable, Father's occupation, was next studied in relation to two other family background variables, Father's education and Mother's education. The average correlation among these three variables across countries was determined and the average correlation of each of the three with Reading Comprehension score. (Where averages across countries were used, these were generally based upon the following nine countries for which data had been received relatively early: Chile, England, Finland, Hungary, the Netherlands, New Zealand, Scotland, Sweden, and the United States.) On the basis of this, regression weights were established for combining the three into a composite socioeconomic measure that would on average give the most effective prediction of Reading Comprehension score. The weighting was in the ratio: 0.25 for Father's occupation, 0.06 for Father's education and 0.12 for Mother's education.

These three variables were now combined into a single composite socioeconomic status variable using the above weights, and for each country the correlations of this variable with other relevant variables as well as with Reading Comprehension score were determined. These correlations entered into further analyses to be described later on.

The second composite that was examined was one involving availability of reading materials in the student's home. There were four questions to which each student in Populations II and IV responded that provided information relating to this one central notion, and three for students in Population I. In all three groups, each student was asked whether a dictionary was available and used in his home, how many books there were in his home, and whether a daily newspaper was regularly received in his home or read by him. In Populations II and IV, an additional question was asked on number of magazines received. Each of these indicators had its own simple correlation with reading achievement, and the correlations were uniformly positive. In the case of these four indicators, a single set of weights was determined for combining the four variables as predictors of reading achievement. The weights were arrived at by pooling data from the first nine countries for which data became available. Pooling the evidence across these nine countries, it was found that in Population II the optimal combination gave a weight of one to the dictionary, a weight of four to the number of books, a weight of one to the magazines, and a weight of one to the presence or absence of a newspaper. The weights for Population IV differed only in that books got a weight of three. These were the weights that were appropriately applied to standardized measures of these four indicators of availability of reading material. Thus, a composite variable was generated using weights that represented an optimal composite pooled over the nine countries, and this became the second pooled predictor of reading achievement.

Using Population II and the same nine countries, a third composite predictor was generated by examination of several items relating to the kinds of interest the parent was alleged to have shown in his child's education. There were three questions, one relating to parent's expressed interest in school, one to encouragement given the child to read, and one to encouragement to the child to visit museums. It turned out that on the average an optimal combination for Population II was to give double weight to the question relating to expressed interest and single weight to the question relating to encouragement to read. The question relating to encouraging the child to visit museums contributed no independent prediction of Reading Comprehension score. This composite served as an indicator of parental interest in the child's schooling and learning for Populations I and II. For Population IV, the best indicator was the one item on museums.

A fourth subset of questionnaire responses seemed to constitute a further rational group. The questions asked whether the parents helped the child with his homework, whether they typically corrected his speaking, and whether they typically corrected his writing when he made errors in it. The zero-order correlation of each of these variables with reading achievement was studied across the set of nine countries. Of the three, the only one that showed any consistent relationship to Reading Comprehension score in Population II was the question about helping with homework. In Population II, the correlation of this variable with reading achievement was uniformly negative. In every country, it was found that the children who reported that their parents helped them with their homework

Table 6.1. *Correlation of Background Variables with Reading Comprehension Score*

	Belgium (Fl)	Belgium (Fr)	Chile	Eng-land	Fin-land	Hun-gary	India	Iran
Population I								
1. SES (Father's occupation)	.08	.28	.12	.35	.22	.39	.00	.28
2. Reading resources	.06	.28	.05	.32	.33	.31	.00	.22
3. Parental interest	.08	−.05	−.02	.15	.03	.14	.12	.23
4. Parental help	−.24	.00	−.06	.07	−.08	−.04	.03	.07
5. Age	.02	.12	−.01	.12	.23	.05	−.08	.09
6. Sex (M = 1, F = 2)	.01	.02	.02	.07	.02	−.01	−.04	.07
7. No. of siblings	.02	−.17	−.04	−.20	−.14	−.22	.09	−.11
Population II								
1. SES (Occup. and Educ.)	.18	.24	.36	.40	.36	.38	.08	.20
2. Reading resources	.25	.26	.33	.41	.39	.32	.07	.13
3. Parental interest	−.01	.04	.12	.18	.05	.17	.07	.07
4. Parental help	−.15	−.07	−.05	−.14	−.10	−.11	−.11	−.01
5. Age	.04	.02	.14	.09	.06	.01	.04	.03
6. Sex (M = 1, F = 2)	.05	.17	−.12	.10	.00	.02	.02	−.03
7. No. of siblings	.00	−.02	−.20	−.23	−.14	−.22	.05	−.05
Population IV								
1. SES (Occup. and Educ.)	.22	.16	.25	.06	.03	.25	.08	.18
2. Reading resources	.23	.16	.26	.08	.07	.14	.10	.17
3. Parental interest	.25	.15	.08	.12	−.05	.04	−.01	−.01
4. Parental help	−.05	−.02	−.06	−.03	−.08	−.07	−.08	−.04
5. Age	−.20	−.22	−.25	−.10	−.32	−.04	−.09	−.15
6. Sex (M = 1, F = 2)	.17	.02	−.16	.08	−.06	−.02	.15	.08
7. No. of siblings	−.06	.05	−.04	−.04	.03	−.02	.04	.01

tended to get poorer reading scores than those who reported that their parents seldom or never provided this type of help. For Population IV, the variable became a composite in which help with homework was weighted two and correct speaking was weighted one. This variable then served to represent the construct of parental participation in instruction of the child, and became a fourth component of the background data.

THE CORRELATION OF PREDICTORS WITH ACHIEVEMENT MEASURES

In addition to the above four composites, there were several single variables available as predictors of reading achievement for the

Table 6.1. (*Cont.*)

	Israel	Italy	Nether-lands	New Zealand	Scot-land	Sweden	United States	Median Corre-lation
Population I								
SES (Father's occupation)	.41	.20	.30	—	.35	.22	.33	.28
Reading resources	.32	.25	.23	—	.34	.25	.28	.26
Parental interest	.05	.11	.10	—	.08	−.04	.08	.08
Parental help	−.01	−.03	−.02	—	−.05	−.03	−.07	−.03
Age	−.07	.04	.14	—	.16	.17	.01	.06
Sex (M = 1, F = 2)	.05	.02	−.05	—	.06	.06	.06	−.02
No. of siblings	−.41	−.03	−.04	—	−.22	−.05	−.17	−.12
Population II								
SES (Occup. and Educ.)	.49	.23	.31	.27	.37	.28	.38	.31
Reading resources	.32	.24	.22	.26	.41	.33	.35	.32
Parental interest	.06	.05	.11	.15	.26	.06	.11	.07
Parental help	−.02	−.07	−.08	−.17	−.06	−.07	−.20	−.08
Age	−.05	.10	.07	.10	.11	.12	−.01	.06
Sex (M = 1, F = 2)	−.03	.02	−.03	.02	−.07	.06	.04	.02
No. of siblings	−.17	−.07	−.08	−.16	−.24	−.09	−.11	−.11
Population IV								
SES (Occup. and Educ.)	.28	.17	.03	.11	.12	.10	.36	.16
Reading resources	.16	.16	.10	.16	.10	.17	.30	.16
Parental interest	.15	.01	.08	.05	.05	.05	.16	.05
Parental help	.06	−.07	−.05	−.02	−.14	−.15	−.15	−.06
Age	−.06	−.22	.03	−.25	−.11	.08	−.18	−.15
Sex (M = 1, F = 2)	.10	.05	.04	.12	−.06	−.03	.07	.05
No. of siblings	−.12	−.15	.02	−.07	−.03	.00	−.08	−.03

members of this population of youngsters. These consisted of the child's age and sex, and his number of siblings. In Table 6.1, the correlation coefficients for each of the predictor composites or single variables against Reading Comprehension score are displayed country by country. The median correlation across the set of countries is also shown. The two background variables that served as the most effective predictors of reading achievement were the socioeconomic composite on the one hand and the reading resources composite on the other. The composite describing parental interest in general showed modest validity, but much less than the first two. The fourth cluster of predictors, identified as active parental participation in teaching, showed a negative relationship in every one of the countries in

Populations II and IV, and the correlations were generally negative in Population I. It would appear that help with the child's educational efforts tends to occur in proportion to its being needed, and that it is the poor achiever rather than the good achiever who receives special parental help. In this sense, it is possible that the response to this item should be thought of as a current description of the student rather than as a predictor variable. However, it certainly appears from these data that there is no tendency for help by the parent to be predictive of good achievement on the part of a child, at least within the domain of reading.

Age is necessarily not a very significant variable for Populations I and II, which were defined as 10-year-olds and 14-year-olds respectively. The generally small positive correlations can be considered to represent the increment in ability that takes place within a single year of the age span. In Population IV, the correlation of reading score with age is quite consistently negative across the set of countries, showing that the tendency for the more able young person to progress more rapidly through the educational system is a very general phenomenon, not limited by national boundaries.

Correlations of Reading Comprehension score with sex are small and inconsistent from country to country. There has been, in the United States at least, an accumulation of evidence indicating that girls progress more rapidly in reading than do boys, and the results of this study for the United States support this result. These results also show a superiority of girls in a majority of countries—11 of 14 in Population I, nine of 15 in Population II, and ten of 15 in Population IV. However, in a small number of countries the trend is reversed and the median correlation is very small indeed.

Family size tends to show a negative correlation with reading achievement in most countries for Populations I and II. Exceptions are Flemish-speaking Belgium and India. Negative correlations of 0.2 or more appear in Chile, England, Hungary, Israel, and Scotland. The negative relationship is difficult to interpret in Population IV, in which a substantial degree of selectivity has operated.

A further step in the analysis was to determine how effectively the variables in combination would predict reading achievement. This analysis was limited to those variables which seemed to predict with some consistency across all of the countries and for which the correlations were of appreciable size. Analysis was made using the socioeconomic composite, the reading resources composite, the parental interest composite, the variable of parental help with homework and number of siblings. In Table 6.2 are displayed the regression loadings applicable to each of these five predictors, and the multiple correlations resulting from this composite prediction. It will be noted that the dominant predictors are socioeconomic status and reading materials in the home. In some countries it is one and in some countries it is the other that has the higher validity and consequently is the dominant variable in the regression equation. In general, the variable of parents' helping with homework is the next most important as a predictor, but comes in with a negative weight, indicating that parental help is an unfavorable rather than a favorable sign as far as achievement is concerned. The unique contribution of expressed interest in the youngster's schooling is typically fairly small and there are a number of countries in which it disappears entirely as having any independent contribution to make in the prediction process.

The level of prediction that is possible from these indicators varies rather substantially from country to country. For Population I the range of multiple correlations was from 0.142 to 0.543. Lowest correlations were obtained in Chile and India. Since, as will be seen in a later chapter, general reading level was rather low in these countries, it is possible that the responses of 10-year-olds to a questionnaire that they had to read were quite undependable. The high correlation for Israel can be understood in terms of the heterogeneity of Israel's population in terms of geographical origin. In Population II, multiple correlations range from 0.175 to 0.538, with India giving the lowest value and Israel the highest. The failure of the socioeconomic index and the index of reading resources to differentiate in India is noteworthy. Responses to the questionnaire indicate that the average socioeconomic level is lowest and the typical resources for reading least of any of the countries participating in the study. However, there was a good deal of variability among pupils in the reported economic and educational level of the home. In spite of this variability, reading level could not be predicted from these factors.

Multiple correlations for Population IV were generally low. Since education at this level has been quite selective in most countries, and since it has probably been true that a student from a poor family had to be especially outstanding if he was to overcome the cultural and economic barriers and pursue a pre-university education, it is hardly surprising that economic factors fail to predict. The one country that still shows a substantial correlation is the United States,

Table 6.2. *Regression Weights and Multiple Correlations for Background Variables*

	Belgium (Fl)	Belgium (Fr)	Chile	England	Finland	Hungary	India	Iran
Population I								
1. Father's occupation	.06	.22	.11	.26	.12	.29	.00	.23
2. Reading resources	.04	.22	.03	.23	.28	.15	−.02	.14
3. Parental interest	.08	−.08	−.03	.04	−.01	.06	.12	.18
4. Parental help	−.24	−.02	−.07	.02	−.11	−.08	.00	.01
5. No. of siblings	.01	−.15	−.03	−.11	−.11	−.12	.09	−.07
R^2	.072	.150	.020	.196	.141	.197	.022	.14⊄
R	.268	.395	.142	.442	.375	.448	.146	.38⊄
Population II								
1. Socioeconomic status	.13	.19	.24	.27	.24	.28	.07	.19
2. Reading resources	.22	.22	.19	.29	.28	.18	.06	.07
3. Parental interest	−.06	.00	.03	.03	.00	.07	.07	.06
4. Parental help	−.14	−.13	−.10	−.15	−.15	−.17	−.14	−.08
5. No. of siblings	−.02	−.03	−.12	−.13	−.08	−.10	.04	−.05
R^2	.101	.114	.181	.281	.223	.216	.031	.05⊄
R	.315	.333	.425	.528	.475	.468	.175	.23⊄
Population IV								
1. Socioeconomic status	.13	.10	.18	.02	.03	.26	.07	.13
2. Reading resources	.13	.10	.19	.06	.08	.07	.09	.14
3. Parental interest	.18	.10	.01	.11	−.05	.01	−.01	−.05
4. Parental help	−.11	−.06	−.14	−.06	−.09	−.15	−.11	−.07
5. No. of siblings	−.07	.02	−.03	−.04	.02	.01	.03	−.01
R^2	.112	.048	.104	.022	.017	.085	.025	.05⊄
R	.335	.222	.324	.151	.134	.292	.156	.22⊄

where the majority of youth complete secondary education. The correlation there is 0.460, but in other countries the maximum prediction from this set of five variables does not go above 0.335.

In addition to the background variables, there are, as already indicated, a number of other variables that describe the individual as he exists at the present time. These variables also can be grouped into logical clusters and the clusters treated as single composite variables in indicating their relationship to current reading performance. The clusters and the individual variables serve to describe the good reader, but should not really be thought of as predictors of reading achievement.

One set of variables available for Populations II and IV more or

	Israel	Italy	Nether-lands	New Zealand	Scot-land	Sweden	United States	Median
~ulation I								
Father's occupation	.31	.12	.26	—	.26	.16	.26	.22
Reading resources	.23	.19	.17	—	.24	.20	.22	.20
Parental interest	−.12	.03	.01	—	.02	−.05	.02	.02
Parental help	−.06	−.07	−.05	—	−.07	−.03	−.07	−.06
No. of siblings	−.25	−.11	−.06	—	−.15	−.04	−.12	−.11
R^2	.296	.093	.121	—	.212	.088	.175	.144
R	.543	.309	.350	—	.461	.298	.419	.378
~ulation II								
Socioeconomic status	.38	.18	.26	.20	.22	.21	.29	.22
Reading resources	.16	.19	.16	.19	.28	.28	.25	.19
Parental interest	−.05	−.03	.07	.10	.11	.00	.05	.03
Parental help	−.12	−.13	−.13	−.20	−.13	−.12	−.23	−.13
No. of siblings	−.16	−.13	−.05	−.10	−.13	−.05	−.07	−.08
R^2	.291	.113	.139	.169	.261	.164	.258	.169
R	.538	.331	.373	.413	.512	.406	.508	.413
~ulation IV								
Socioeconomic status	.25	.14	.01	.08	.11	.10	.28	.11
Reading resources	.08	.14	.09	.14	.09	.16	.20	.10
Parental interest	.06	−.04	.09	.03	−.05	.04	.09	.03
Parental help	−.05	−.11	−.10	−.06	−.18	−.20	−.20	−.11
No. of siblings	.01	−.14	.02	−.07	−.04	.01	−.05	−.01
R^2	.091	.075	.022	.038	.052	.069	.210	.052
R	.302	.273	.149	.196	.228	.266	.460	.228

less parallels the background variables relating to socioeconomic status. It includes the level of occupation to which the individual aspires and the amount of additional education he hopes to attain. The evidence on aspiration originally existed as a category of occupation to which the individual aspired. This resulted from coding the specific occupation into the same groupings that were used for describing Father's occupation. The information was then reduced to an empirically scaled variables using the same weights for the young person's aspiration as had resulted from empirically scaling the results for Father's occupation. The variable becomes in a sense, then, the degree to which the occupation to which the student aspires is one that has produced able readers as offspring

Table 6.3. *Correlations of Expected Socioeconomic Status with Reading Comprehension Score*

Country	Expected Occupation		Expected Education		Composite	
	Population II	Population IV	Population II	Population IV	Population II	Population IV
Belgium (Fl)	.29	.37	.18	.32	.27	.39
Belgium (Fr)	.13	.15	.38	.31	.34	.31
Chile	.19	.10	.14	.18	.20	.20
England	.38	−.04	.44	.08	.48	.03
Finland	.41	.04	.43	.18	.48	.15
Hungary	.46	.22	.45	.32	.49	.33
India	.03	−.05	.07	.03	.06	.00
Iran	.04	.11	.20	.11	.17	.14
Israel	.25	.15	.33	.24	.37	.25
Italy	.12	.07	.30	.18	.27	.17
Netherlands	.43	.09	.37	.03	.46	.07
New Zealand	.40	.06	.30	.08	.40	.09
Scotland	.43	.10	.46	.27	.51	.26
Sweden	.30	.17	.37	.26	.40	.27
United States	.21	.28	.26	.29	.29	.35
Median	.29	.10	.33	.18	.37	.20

in the past. This variable of occupational level may be combined with the variable of educational expectation into a composite variable that we may call Socioeconomic expectation. The weight for combining the two variables was based upon the average correlation of each with reading in Population II averaged over the 15 countries and was chosen so that it would maximize the prediction. This uniform combination, which turned out to be three times Expected occupation plus four times Expected education, was then applied to each of the countries in order to determine the correlation of this socioeconomic expectation composite with reading achievement. The results are shown in Table 6.3 in which one can see, country by country, the correlation of the two separate components and the correlation of the weighted composite based upon the combination of them.

Clearly, in Population II, the individual's educational plans are appreciably related to the level of his performance on the reading tasks, and his occupational plans are also reflected though to a somewhat lesser extent. There is, in general, a higher correlation between the individual's expectations on socioeconomic level and his current reading than there is between parental socioeconomic status and current reading. This is a natural and rational finding. The reading score, after all, characterizes the specific individual; it should be more closely related to his own plans and aspirations than it is to some variable that characterizes his family background.

The correlations among students in Population II appear to be highest in the European countries and countries with a history of selective education. Where educational programs are differentiated at a fairly early age, and where the future educational (and occupational) possibilities are to a considerable extent specified as a result of that early allocation to a particular program, the reading score, which represents a very general index of educational achievement and is substantially correlated with educational program, becomes a good indicator of what the individual can and does expect for his future. The correlations are lowest in developing countries—perhaps because of reading problems on the part of the students that upset the meaning of their questionnaire responses.

At the level of Population IV, the correlations in most countries are markedly reduced. The median correlation for the composite index drops from 0.37 to 0.18. This is without question a function of the selection that has taken place in most countries. The selection has reduced the range both of reading talent and of vocational and educational expectations, by dropping off the lower levels of each, and factors other than reading ability become dominant in determining what type of occupation or future education the remaining students aspire to. In a few countries, however, the situation is reversed, and the correlations are higher in Population IV. Thus, in the United States the correlation goes up from 0.29 to 0.35. One may speculate that in an undifferentiated educational system in which most students continue through secondary education, plans and expectations become clarified during the secondary school years, so that they match level of ability more closely at age 17+ than they did at age 14.

A second set of variables that describe the individual as he exists at the time of testing consists of his choices of materials to read in books and magazines, his pattern of reading the daily paper, and his preferences for television viewing. For each type of book or magazine reading, the student was asked whether he liked to read this type of material (1) Not at all, (2) Occasionally, or (3) Frequently. His score (1, 2 or 3) for each was correlated with Reading Comprehension

Table 6.4. *Correlations of Choice of Types of Reading Material with Reading Comprehension Score*

Type of Reading Material	Population II		Population IV	
	Range	Median	Range	Median
Adventure	.07 to .27	+.15	−.14 to .19	−.01
History and biography	−.02 to .24	+.18	−.02 to .19	+.12
Science/technical	−.02 to .21	+.05	.00 to .16	+.11
Science fiction	.03 to .38	+.18	−.06 to .17	+.06
Travel and exploration	.02 to .31	+.13	−.02 to .08	+.01
Current events	.04 to .34	+.15	.02 to .20	+.08
Mystery and detective	.03 to .17	+.11	−.15 to .10	−.02
Art	−.14 to .29	+.01	−.08 to .25	+.08
Politics and economics	−.01 to .18	+.03	−.10 to .15	+.08
Philosophy and religion	−.13 to .13	−.01	−.11 to .18	+.12
Sports	−.18 to .06	−.07	−.14 to −.03	−.10
Love stories	−.12 to .13	−.05	−.20 to .04	−.10
Humor	.12 to .40	+.23	−.09 to .15	+.06
Myths and legends	−.02 to .28	+.18	−.02 to .16	+.09
Poetry	−.15 to .17	−.01	−.03 to .22	+.06
Movie and music celebrities	−.17 to .06	−.01	−.16 to .15	−.06
School stories	−.11 to .22	−.04	−.17 to .00	−.06

score. The results are summarized in Table 6.4. In Population II, liking for most types of reading is associated with good reading ability, though sports, love stories and school stories show small negative correlations on the average. The types that are most positively correlated with Reading Comprehension score are, in order, (1) humor, (2) history and biography, science fiction, and myths and legends, and (3) adventure and current events. By the end of the secondary school, the pattern has changed somewhat, though the same categories show up as negatively correlated with Comprehension score, to wit, sports, love stories and school stories. History and biography, technical science, and philosophy and religion now show the strongest positive correlations.

On the basis of the first group of countries analyzed, average correlations were determined for the correlation of liking for a given type of reading with Comprehension score. Using these average correlations, a prediction equation was developed for predicting Reading Comprehension score. The best weighted combination for Population II was:

Table 6.5. *Correlations of Practice of Reading Different Sections of Newspaper with Reading Comprehension Score*

Section of Paper	Population II		Population IV	
	Range	Median	Range	Median
News	.05 to .17	+.13	−.05 to .16	+.07
Sports	−.10 to .02	−.04	−.15 to .02	−.08
Comment about news	−.05 to .14	−.01	−.08 to .18	+.06
Articles about home	−.15 to −.01	−.08	−.12 to .05	−.06
Movie, TV, play reviews	−.09 to .06	−.04	−.08 to .13	+.04
Music and art reviews	−.08 to .05	−.01	−.06 to .17	+.02
Book reviews	−.09 to .13	+.03	−.05 to .18	+.07
Comics	.05 to .33	+.17	−.02 to .13	+.08
Science articles	.10 to 22	+.17	−.04 to .16	+.09

0.08 (Adventure) + 0.09 (History and biography) + 0.12 (Science fiction) + 0.06 (Current events) + 0.18 (Humor) + 0.08 (Myths and legends)

This equation was applied in each country to determine the correlations of a composite expression of reading preferences with Reading Comprehension score.

A similar analysis was made of the sections of the newspaper and the correlations across countries for the different sections are summarized in Table 6.5. On the basis of these average values, it appeared that, in Population II, four sections of the newspaper for which the individual had to report that he tended to read that section with some regularity were predictive of Reading Comprehension. The four sections were: news, comics and science articles with positive correlations and articles about home with a negative one. Taking the values averaged across countries, the optimum combination of the four gave weights as follows:

0.11 (News) − 0.08 (Home) + 0.16 (Comics) + 0.14 (Science)

This provided a composite newspaper reading index, which, added to the general reading index, provided two cues as to reading behavior in the sense of its relationship to reading achievement.

One could combine the two into a single composite score, and this was done for Population II in each country. Table 6.6 shows the correlation of each of the two reading indices separately with Reading Comprehension and the correlation of the combination of the two.

Table 6.6. *Correlations of Reading Preference Composites with Reading Comprehension Score. Population II*

Country	Comprehension vs. Book and Magazine Composite	Comprehension vs. Newspaper Composite	Book and Magazine vs. Newspaper	Comprehension vs. Combined Composites
Belgium (Fl)	.26	.18	.27	.28
Belgium (Fr)	.28	.12	.31	.28
Chile	.40	.38	.46	.46
England	.46	.30	.33	.49
Finland	.25	.31	.26	.36
Hungary	.32	.22	.28	.35
India	.30	.22	.34	.32
Iran	.18	.20	.34	.23
Israel	.32	.28	.36	.36
Italy	.24	.22	.29	.29
Netherlands	.35	.17	.28	.36
New Zealand	.32	.25	.28	.36
Scotland	.50	.31	.29	.53
Sweden	.30	.21	.24	.33
United States	.30	.21	.26	.33
Median	.30	.22	.29	.35

It is clear that among 14-year-olds one can with considerable uniformity account for an appreciable amount of Reading Comprehension score in terms of the amount and type of material that the individual says he reads, or, conversely, the amount and type of material that the individual says he reads is to a considerable extent a function of the individual's level of Reading Comprehension.

Several additional expressions of attitude were obtained from each individual at the same time that the Reading Comprehension score was obtained. At each age level a series of items, some phrased as statements, some as questions, was scored to give a score for Liking of school and Motivation to achieve. A further set of questions elicited the pupil's perception of his school as open and permissive or as structured and controlled. In connection with the testing in Science, questionnaires were provided to yield at each population level a score on Interest in Science. For Populations II and IV a second score expressed the individual's opinion of the importance of Science and its value to mankind. Finally, in those countries testing in Literature an appraisal was made of literary interest. (See

Table 6.7. *Correlations of Student Attitudes and Perceptions with Reading Comprehension Score. Population I*

Country	Liking for School	School Motivation	School Environment	Science Interest
Belgium (Fl)	.16	.18	.13	−.02
Belgium (Fr)	.09	.25	.02	−.04
Chile	.38	.32	−.14	−.23
England	.17	.29	.04	−.03
Finland	.16	.25	−.14	.04
Hungary	.14	.19	.11	−.04
India	.44	.29	.05	−.09
Iran	.34	.29	−.21	.11
Israel	.15	.28	.09	−.07
Italy	.15	.21	.12	.01
Netherlands	.19	.15	.04	.02
Scotland	.12	.31	.01	−.11
Sweden	.08	.16	.05	−.02
United States	.08	.33	.10	−.03
Median	.16	.28	.04	−.03

Volumes I and II in the present series.) We will now examine the relationships of these measures to individual level of Reading Comprehension.

The data for Population I are shown in Table 6.7. At this age level, expression of liking for school typically shows a slight correlation with Reading Comprehension score, and motivation to do well in school a more substantial one. The median correlations are 0.16 and 0.28 respectively. Neither the school environment score nor the expression of interest in Science show any consistent relationship to reading performance.

Results for Population II are shown in Table 6.8. All five of the attitude measures, as well as the descriptive picture of the school, show small but rather consistent positive correlations with reading achievement. The good reader tends to like school, to be motivated to achieve, to be interested in Science and/or Literature (at this age the two interests tend to show a positive correlation), and to consider Science valuable and important for mankind. A weighted composite of attitudes is somewhat more predictive than any of them separately, yielding a correlation of 0.26 when based on the median correlations. Furthermore, at this age level, the better reader tends to see his school as more rigid and authoritarian than does the

Table 6.8. *Correlations of Student Attitudes and Perceptions with Reading Comprehension Score. Population II*

Country	Liking for School	School Motivation	School Environment	Science Interest	Value of Science	Literary Interest
Belgium (Fl)	.15	.16	.03	.02	.06	.14
Belgium (Fr)	.11	−.01	.11	.20	.04	.24
Chile	.12	.16	.03	.10	.34	.08
England	.20	.10	.30	.21	.17	.17
Finland	.14	.10	.18	.17	.34	.12
Hungary	.19	.10	.25	.19	.40	—
India	.30	.12	.05	−.10	.24	—
Iran	.03	.09	.02	.05	.11	.14
Israel	−.12	−.04	.37	—	—	—
Italy	.11	.10	.19	.13	.17	.14
Netherlands	.08	.03	.26	.07	.14	—
New Zealand	.19	.18	.28	.18	.22	.16
Scotland	.27	.17	.41	.28	.20	—
Sweden	.23	.20	.20	.12	.24	.13
United States	.17	.08	.33	—	—	.19
Median	.15	.10	.20	.13	.20	.14

poorer reader. It will be seen in the next chapter that this difference is in part at least a difference between schools, and that this descriptive evaluation is related to the category of school or program in which the student is enrolled.

We turn next to Population IV, the results for which are shown in Table 6.9. As has been observed for other variables, most of these correlations are lower than in Population II, again reflecting the reduced range of variation in this end-of-secondary-school population. School interest and motivation no longer appear to differentiate levels of reading ability, but modest relationships continue to appear for interest in Science and perception of Science as important and valuable, and also for literary interest. Based on the median correlations, a composite of attitude would correlate about 0.22 with Reading Comprehension score.

THE REGRESSION ANALYSES

A second somewhat different type of analysis was applied to the data for individual students. In this analysis, as described in Chapter

Table 6.9. *Correlations of Student Attitudes and Perceptions with Reading Comprehension Score. Population IV*

Country	Liking for School	School Motiva- tion	School Environ- ment	Science Interest	Value of Science	Literary Interest
Belgium (Fl)	.14	−.04	.14	.12	.07	.37
Belgium (Fr)	.05	−.06	.11	.10	.21	.20
Chile	−.02	−.07	.11	.14	.23	.10
England	.12	.07	.17	.09	.12	.18
Finland	−.02	−.06	.06	.06	.17	.06
Hungary	.10	.00	.11	.08	.15	—
India	.13	.01	.14	.02	.13	—
Iran	.00	.04	.10	.00	−.06	.14
Israel	−.03	−.11	.11	—	—	—
Italy	−.06	−.03	.18	.03	.15	.15
Netherlands	.08	.08	.12	.10	.19	—
New Zealand	.06	.03	.10	.10	.08	.16
Scotland	.03	.02	.13	.18	.16	—
Sweden	.17	.07	.12	.10	.09	.07
United States	.18	.08	.18	—	—	.20
Median	.06	.01	.12	.10	.15	.16

5, the variables were grouped by blocks, and a multiple regression analysis was carried out adding each block in turn. The four blocks with which this chapter will be concerned can be characterized approximately as follows:

Block 1: Home and student background variables,
Block 2: School placement variables,
Block 3: School treatment, or learning conditions variables, and
Block 4: Personal attributes, or "kindred" variables.

Each block was added in turn to the set of variables being used for prediction, and as many variables from the block were included as added to the prediction at the specified significance level. The multiple correlation was determined after the addition of each block, and the percent of predicted variance added by the block was determined.

Population I

The results for Population I are shown in the first section of Table 6.10. The median multiple correlation based on Block 1 alone was

Table 6.10. *Multiple Correlations and Added Percents of Variance for Four Blocks of Variables. Population I*

Country	Home Background, Age and Sex		School and Program Type		School Variables		Kindred Variables	
	R	%Added Variance	R	%Added Variance	R	%Added Variance	R	%Added Variance
Belgium (Fl)	.13	1.7	.13	0.0	.36	11.6	.47	9.2
Belgium (Fr)	.41	16.7	.42	1.1	.60	18.4	.62	2.6
Chile	.12	1.4	.16	1.2	.33	8.3	.47	11.4
England	.47	22.1	.47	0.4	.49	1.5	.56	7.4
Finland	.42	17.7	.42	0.0	.45	2.8	.53	7.3
Hungary	.43	18.7	.44	0.3	.48	3.8	.53	5.6
India	.12	1.6	.14	0.3	.41	14.9	.55	14.0
Iran	.29	8.7	.42	9.1	.50	7.2	.55	5.3
Israel	.50	25.4	.52	1.9	.56	3.6	.61	5.7
Italy	.31	9.6	.31	0.2	.38	4.4	.42	3.8
Netherlands	.33	11.1	.36	1.6	.41	4.0	.51	9.7
Scotland	.49	23.7	.49	0.3	.51	2.3	.58	7.5
Sweden	.34	11.4	.34	0.3	.38	2.9	.43	3.7
United States	.44	19.8	.46	2.0	.50	3.8	.56	6.2
Median	.38	14.0	.42	.04	.46	3.9	.54	6.8

0.38, with 14% of Reading Comprehension variance accounted for. Block 1 included five variables: (1) Father's occupation, empirically scaled to maximize approximately prediction of Reading Comprehension score, (2) Number of siblings, (3) Age, (4) Sex, and (5) Reading resources in the home, defined as a composite index of availability of books, newspapers and dictionary. As indicated earlier in this chapter, the greater part of the prediction was carried by Father's occupation and the index of reading resources. These can be thought of as somewhat crude indices of the economic and cultural level of the home.

In Population I, adding the second block, which at this level consisted of only one variable, to wit, a categorization of type of school, added very little to the possible prediction. Since there is, in most countries, little differentiation of schools or school program for 10-year-olds, it is hardly surprising that this variable was of little consequence.

The third block was composed of a number of variables presumably describing the school and its procedures. Inclusion of this block

Table 6.10. *Population II (Cont.)*

Country	Home Background, Age and Sex		School and Program Type		School Variables		Kindred Variables	
	R	% Added Variance	R	% Added Variance	R	% Added Variance	R	% Added Variance
Belgium (Fl)	.27	7.5	.43	10.7	.52	9.3	.58	6.2
Belgium (Fr)	.33	11.2	.51	14.5	.60	10.3	.66	7.2
Chile	.45	20.1	.51	5.9	.57	6.6	.62	6.0
England	.52	27.3	.64	13.7	.66	2.6	.71	7.2
Finland	.45	20.3	.58	13.4	.62	4.3	.68	8.8
Hungary	.43	18.6	.47	3.9	.52	4.0	.60	9.7
India	.12	1.4	.21	3.1	.38	9.7	.45	5.8
Iran	.25	6.1	.31	3.2	.40	6.6	.45	4.1
Israel	.50	25.2	.63	13.9	.66	4.3	.69	4.9
Italy	.32	10.4	.48	12.4	.51	3.2	.58	7.6
Netherlands	.35	12.5	.58	20.7	.61	3.9	.68	8.7
New Zealand	.37	13.5	.56	17.6	.63	8.2	.68	7.5
Scotland	.51	26.1	.62	12.3	.65	3.9	.71	8.5
Sweden	.40	16.1	.40	0.0	.44	2.9	.58	14.7
United States	.47	22.1	.50	3.4	.57	6.5	.65	10.6
Median	.40	16.1	.51	12.3	.57	4.3	.65	7.5

raised the typical multiple correlation to 0.46 and added about 4% to the variance accounted for. However, the only variable in the block to receive a consistent regression weight across the set of countries was Grade level in which the student was placed, and one could well argue that this really belonged in the previous block as a school placement variable, rather than appearing as an aspect of schooling. What it seems to say is merely that the less able 10-year-olds who have fallen behind their classmates do less well on a reading test than those who have made normal, or possibly accelerated progress. All 14 of the remaining variables in this block receive weights that are positive in some countries, negative in others. The nearest to a consistent weighting is for the presence of a library or book corner in the classroom. This receives a positive weight in six countries, negative in one. All in all, then, there is little evidence that any of the variables of school organization or school procedure makes any difference as far as individual reading performance is concerned.

The fourth block is composed of five variables that represent

Table 6.10. *Population IV (Cont.)*

Country	Home Background, Age and Sex		School and Program Type		School Variables		Kindred Variables	
	R	% Added Variance	R	% Added Variance	R	% Added Variance	R	% Added Variance
Belgium (Fl)	.36	12.7	.56	18.5	.59	3.4	.65	7.7
Belgium (Fr)	.27	7.2	.39	8.4	.49	9.0	.54	5.1
Chile	.39	14.9	.45	4.9	.50	5.1	.54	4.0
England	.15	2.4	.20	1.8	.30	4.6	.40	7.6
Finland	.34	11.5	.37	2.3	.40	2.3	.47	5.9
Hungary	.26	6.9	.39	8.5	.45	4.8	.52	6.9
India	.20	4.0	.25	2.2	.33	4.7	.36	2.0
Iran	.23	5.5	.23	0.0	.36	7.6	.38	1.4
Israel	.29	8.6	.53	19.4	.66	15.2	.69	3.7
Italy	.31	9.6	.42	7.8	.47	5.0	.50	2.9
Netherlands	.10	1.0	.31	7.4	.36	4.8	.40	3.1
New Zealand	.30	9.0	.32	1.6	.35	1.9	.44	6.7
Scotland	.20	4.0	.23	1.4	.30	3.5	.45	11.3
Sweden	.21	4.2	.43	14.0	.45	1.8	.50	4.9
United States	.42	17.5	.51	8.0	.53	2.9	.58	5.2
Median	.27	7.2	.39	7.4	.45	4.7	.50	5.1

current characteristics of the individual. They *may* have been influenced by the nature of his schooling, by the character of his home background, or more likely by both. They may interact with his reading skill, being either cause or effect or both. Because they are concomitant variables, rather than clearly either causes or results, they have been designated "kindred" variables. The five that were included in this block for Population I were:

1. Reported liking for school, based on response to a series of statements such as "I generally dislike my schoolwork,"
2. Motivation to do well in school, based on response to a series of statements or questions such as "Is it important to you to do well in school?"
3. Reported hours per week devoted to reading for pleasure,
4. Reported hours per week spent watching television, and
5. Report that parents help the student with his school work.

As Table 6.10 indicates, these kindred variables consistently make a modest contribution to prediction, even when they are the last addition to the team of predictors. The median multiple correlation after this block has been added in is 0.54, and the block adds about 7 % to the explained variance. This block is generally more potent than either of the blocks dealing with school treatment. Two of the five variables, Liking for school and School motivation, show positive correlations in every country, and one or both of them always appears with a positive regression weight. Reading for pleasure has a positive correlation in 12 of 14 countries, and a positive regression weight in ten. Hours watching TV appears with a negative correlation in 11 of 13 countries, though the negative correlations are usually small, and with a negative regression weight in ten. Only in Italy does TV watching contribute with a positive weight to prediction of Reading Comprehension score. Parental help with homework, which should perhaps have been included in the first block of home environment variables, shows a negative correlation in ten of 14 countries, and receives a negative regression weight in 11 of 14. Thus, with a fair amount of consistency across countries it is possible to describe the good 10-year-old reader as a youngster who likes school, is strongly motivated to do well in school, manages his school work without parental help, does more than an average amount of free reading and less than an average amount of TV viewing.

How good a prediction would this block provide, if taken entirely by itself? The solution has been worked out for one country, Finland, which is close to the median in the correlations for the variables taken separately. The multiple correlation for the block comes out to be 0.34, which can be compared with 0.42 for home background in Finland and 0.38 as the median value for home background in the set of 14 countries. Thus, the set of kindred variables that we have analyzed is somewhat, but not markedly less effective than home background in predicting level of reading achievement.

Population II
Attention may be turned to the 14-year-olds of Population II. At this level, Block 1 includes the somewhat more complete index of Home background described on page 72, composed of Father's occupation, Father's education and Mother's education. The index of Reading resources has been expanded to include magazines as well as books, newspapers and dictionary. In addition to these, the block includes Age, Sex and Number of siblings. The median multiple correlation based on the background variables of Block 1 is 0.40, slightly higher than for Population I. At both ages, the prediction from Block 1 is

very low for India, rather low for Iran and Flemish-speaking Belgium. Prediction is good in both populations for Israel and for the English-speaking countries.

Block 2, School and Program Type, behaves very differently for Population II than it did for Population I. Whereas at the earlier level it accounted for almost no variance in reading score, by age 14 it accounts on the average for an additional 12% of the variance in reading score. This variance accounted for varies widely, ranging from zero in Sweden (where apparently no differentiation of programs is recognized and differentiation of schools is inconsequential) to almost 21% in the Netherlands. In nine of 15 countries, school or program type adds over 10% to the predicted variance. Taking French-speaking Belgium as a fairly typical example in terms of the predictive role of Block 2, a multiple correlation of 0.49 can be obtained from this block alone.

Clearly, in many countries placement in a particular school or program has by age 14 become a major indicator of educational competence. This was not true four years earlier, but the sorting has taken place at some point during the interim, and the sorting has certainly taken place in large part on the basis of prior demonstration of academic competence. It is, of course, possible that the difference in school environment subsequent to the point of sorting has served to enhance the difference, and that some fraction of the variance in Block 2 should be viewed as an effect of educational treatment. But a large part of it must certainly be considered to represent individual competence demonstrated at the time that placement took place.

Block 3 was composed of 14 school variables that had given promise in preliminary analyses of being able to add to prediction in some or all countries. Collectively, these variables accounted on the average for an additional 4.3% of variance in the reading score. However, as in Population I, the most consistent and potent predictor was Grade in school, which might be considered to belong more appropriately in Block 2. This one variable accounts, on the average, for 2.2% of the added variance in reading score, leaving only 2.1% for the school treatment variables. The most consistent of these is Hours homework per week, which has a positive loading in 11 countries and accounts on the average for another six tenths of a percent of reading score variance. Mother-tongue class size also receives a positive weight in 11 countries, but accounts for less than four tenths of a percent of variance on the average. Number of weeks of schooling per year receives a negative weight in five countries. None of the other variables is entirely consistent from country to country in the sign of its regression weight, and a number divide almost evenly between positive and negative weights. The most consistent are: Group for reading instruction—negative in eight countries, positive in one; Specialist teacher for mother-tongue—positive in five, negative in one; and Urbanness of community—negative in five and positive in one. The general conclusion must be, it appears, that variables of school organization and program have added very little of a consistent nature to the prediction of reading performance.

Block 4 is, once again, made up of the various kindred variables. Its addition boosts the median multiple correlation to 0.65, and contributes a median of 7.5% more to the variance accounted for by the team of predictors. The contribution parallels closely the 6.8% contributed by this block in Population I. The block contains 12 variables, and ten of these are quite consistent contributors, across the set of countries, to the prediction of Reading Comprehension score. The variables, and the direction in which they are weighted to predict, are as follows:

1. Literary interest—negative in five countries.
2. Expected level of education—positive in ten countries.
3. Hours of reading for pleasure—positive in 12 countries, negative in one.
4. Reported home interest in student's schooling—negative in eight countries.
5. Parents help with student's school work—negative in nine countries.
6. Type of expressed reading activities and preferences—positive in 13 countries.
7. Type of reported newspaper reading and preferences—positive in 11 countries.
8. Hours of TV and radio listening—positive in ten countries.
9. Frequency of movie attendance—negative in 12 countries.
10. Choosing "history, travel, nature, scientific developments" as most preferred type of TV program—positive in nine countries.

Some comment is probably in order on (6) and (7) above. These were in each case empirically derived composite scores giving weight to categories of reading (e.g., adventure, history and biography, science fiction, travel and exploration, current events, mystery and detective, humor, myths and legends) which were *generally* found to differentiate the more from the less able readers. Naturally, a variable so designed would have an average tendency to differentiate good from poor readers. However, it would not be necessary that the differentiation be universal, appearing in all countries, and it does appear to be nearly so.

Again one country fairly typical in terms of the regression data has been chosen, in this case New Zealand, and the multiple correlation based only on the kindred variables has been calculated. In this instance the correlation comes out to be 0.50. This is considerably more than the prediction provided by the home and background variables, either specifically for New Zealand or for the median of all the countries. Thus, it appears that the concomitant kindred variables, which are a more complete set at this age, account for a more substantial fraction of the variance as one moves up from Population I to Population II.

Population IV

Finally, we turn to Population IV, the students in the final year of secondary education. The multiple correlation and the variance added by each of the four blocks of predictor variables are shown in the last section of Table 6.10. As one would expect, knowing the extent of selective attrition that has taken place in most countries, the correlations and proportions of variance are substantially lower than at earlier levels. Thus, Block 1 shows a median multiple correlation of 0.27, accounting for only 7.2% of the variance in reading score as compared to 16.1% in Population II. School program and type seem also to have become less effective as predictors in Population IV, the percent of added variance dropping from 12.3 to 7.4. One suspects that the less academic and less selective programs have terminated in many countries and are not represented in Population IV, so that there is less diversity of schools and programs.

The amount of new variance accounted for by school variables is very slightly greater in Population IV than in the earlier groups— 4.7% as compared with 3.9% and 4.3%. However, most of the 15 variables that were examined in this analysis still yield inconsistent results from country to country, showing a mixture of negative and positive regression weights. The only variables that show a clear preponderance in one direction are Hours homework per week (11 positive, one negative) and Proportion of mother-tongue teachers female (seven positive, one negative). Thus, there is very little that one can point to as consistently characterizing the high-achieving school.

The proportion of variance accounted for by kindred variables is less in this group than in the lower-level groups—5.1% as compared with 6.8% and 7.5%. This can again be interpreted as reflecting the greater homogeneity in activities and tastes of those who have persevered to the end of secondary education. The weighting of variables does show a good deal of consistency from country to country, and of congruity with the pattern seen in 14-year-olds. The variables, and the manner in which they were weighted, are as follows:

1. Expressed liking for school—positive in four countries.
2. School motivation score—positive in five, negative in two.
3. Literary interest—positive in six, negative in one.
4. Level of expected occupation—positive in 11 countries, negative in one.
5. Expected level of education—positive in eight, negative in two.
6. Hours of reading for pleasure—positive in 11 countries.
7. Parents correct speech and writing—negative in 14 countries, positive in one.
8. Type of expressed reading activity and preferences—positive in 12 countries.
9. Type of reported newspaper reading and preferences—positive in ten countries.
10. On TV choose history, travel, nature or science programs rather than sports—positive in six countries.

Taking one fairly representative country, in this case the United States, we find that the multiple correlation based on the above ten variables alone is 0.38. This may be taken as fairly representative of the predictive power of the kindred variables considered in isolation. While this is greater than the 0.27 that is typical for the home background composite at this level, it falls well below the value of 0.50 obtained for the kindred composite in Population II, documenting further the reduction in prediction that is possible in the curtailed group remaining at the end of secondary education.

SUMMARY

In this chapter quite a mass of detail has been presented on the factors in the home, in school placement, in school operations, and in other current characteristics of students that are associated with their abilities on a Reading Comprehension test. At this point some attempt at summarizing seems appropriate.

Although there are appreciable variations from country to country, certain general trends stand out. In the first place, it is clear that information about characteristics of the home and community environment in which a youngster has grown up permits a fairly good prediction of his achievement in reading at age 10 and at age 14. The prediction is less effective at the end of secondary education, but this can be understood in most countries as stemming from the fact that a good deal of selection has taken place by the end of secondary education on the basis both of academic ability and economic level, so that those who remain are a select group, not representative of the total population of the country.

In the 10-year-old group, placement in type of school seems to be of no great importance as a predictor. However, with 14-year-olds in many countries a very substantial part of the variation in reading achievement is represented by the type of school or type of program in which the individual is placed. It seems reasonable to think of these variables as representing primarily classification variables rather than treatment variables. That is, assignment to one or another type of school or program is likely to take place on the basis of previously demonstrated ability, so that the differences in achievement of students in the different categories of schools should probably be thought of primarily as an indication of the type of classification that has taken place and only secondarily as a result of the treatment that has been in effect in one school as compared to another. Among those in the final year of secondary education, type of school or program seems to be of less importance in many countries than it was for 14-year-olds, again because the continuing programs are more uniform by the pre-university year, and because a high degree of selection has taken place.

The third general category of variables, and one in which the study was particularly interested, is composed of variables describing schools in terms of their organization, facilities, and treatment of students. The effects of these differences can only be seen clearly after allowance is made for differences in the input of students into different categories of schools. Hence, it becomes necessary to partial out the effects of the previous two kinds of variables, to wit, family and background variables, and the classification effects resulting from assigning students in terms of their previously demonstrated ability. After these effects have been taken care of, very little consistent pattern is found in the school variables associated with differences in achievement. Though certain variables do emerge in single countries, the same variables may appear with a reversed significance in some other country. The number of schools studied in each country is not large enough for one to be confident that the differences from country to country are really stable and meaningful. At this point about the only conclusion that it seems possible to draw is that from among the kinds of school treatment variables on which it was possible to obtain information in a large survey type of study, little emerges that is useful in understanding the progress of students toward higher levels of Reading Comprehension. The same seemed to apply in Science (see Volume I).

Finally, there are a number of other current characteristics of students that tend to be associated with higher levels of reading ability. These are characteristics that should probably be thought of as *concomitants* rather than as either causes or results. They are part of a syndrome or constellation of characteristics that describe the better reader on the one hand as compared with the poorer on the other. Thus, the better reader reads more, reads more in such areas as current events, science, philosophy, and even humor, and reads less in the fields of romance and adventure. The better reader plans to continue his education and aspires to a higher level of occupation in the future. He has certain attitudes that differentiate him, the one that is the most clear cut in the evidence available being a belief in the importance and value of science for human affairs.

It must be confessed that the results of the study provide little guidance for the improvement of the educational enterprise. They point out the very decided importance of the input into any school system in determining its outcomes, but, as in the massive study of schools in the United States included in the Coleman report (1966), they do little to accentuate the importance of differences between schools in their effects upon students. This is not to say that schooling is unimportant. It may merely be that schooling is relatively standardized, so that extreme variations in quality tend not to occur. The results are consistent with the view that more extreme variations occur in home and familial backgrounds, and that the school is an aspect of society that provides more nearly standard experiences and opportunities. However, before accepting this interpretation, the very real limitations of large scale survey data must be considered. In the present study, the evidence on schools and on individuals was obtained largely through questionnaire responses, with all of the problems of communication and cooperation that such questionnaire responses imply. Thus, the largely negative results on school effects may need to be interpreted in part at least as a reflection of the limitations of the methods and the data, as well as indicating the primary importance of the factors outside the school in determining the achievement, either individually or collectively, of the students in a given school.

REFERENCE

Coleman, J. S. *et al. Equality of Educational Opportunity.* (Vols. I and II.) Washington: US Government Printing Office, 1966.

Chapter 7

Factors Associated with School Differences in Reading Achievement

In this chapter attention is turned to the school variables that may be related to differences in average reading achievement of the students rather than the characteristics of single students considered in Chapter 6. These factors include the resources of money, materials and personnel to support a reading program; the characteristics and training of the teachers; the availability of specialized ancillary personnel; and the procedures of instruction, including especially the procedures for adapting the instruction to the needs and characteristics of individual students. Most of the information on characteristics of the school is drawn either from the School Questionnaire completed by some administrative officer of the school or from a pooling of Teacher Questionnaires completed by a sampling of teachers within the school.

Of course, one major determiner of average school achievement is the nature of the student population attending the school. Schools may vary widely in the socioeconomic and ethnic composition of their student body. Furthermore, some types of schools are systematically selective in the students whom they admit. The correlation of average achievement with extra-school variables that stand as surrogates for the capability of the entering student group is in many instances quite substantial. Thus, the correlation of average level of Father's occupation with average level of Reading Comprehension in Population I (10-year-olds) is 0.70 in England, 0.67 in Israel, 0.75 in the United States. It becomes necessary, therefore, to take student input into account, as far as this is possible, in an interpretation of the relationships of school variables to achievement. School variables may be substantially related to input variables, either positively or negatively, and hence show a relationship to reading (positive or negative) as a result of reflecting student input. It is only when input is held constant statistically, as far as is possible, that one can begin to isolate the independent influence of school variables.

Two approaches were used in studying school variables as predictors of Reading Comprehension. The first was to select groups of variables that seemed on an a priori basis to be ones that might well be related to achievement in reading, to organize them in logically related groups, and to look at the correlations of these variables with average reading achievement for the school both before and after partialling out Father's occupation and, in the case of Populations II and IV, Type of school and Type of program. The second approach was through a systematic step-wise regression analysis, as described in Chapter 5. This procedure started with the long, organized list of several hundred variables. Father's occupation and Type of program were partialled out of the correlation of each variable with Reading Comprehension. Then the partial correlations for all countries for a variable were displayed graphically, were examined systematically, and only those variables were retained for regression analysis that met minimum criteria of average size over countries, or of size within the data for single countries.

The regression analysis started with a "School Handicap Score," composed of home environment variables, designed to give as good a representation as possible of student input. The following blocks of variables were then added in turn, to see how much each would add to the prediction of reading achievement:

1. Other home background variables,
2. Type of school—i.e., category or classification,
3. Within-school variables, relating to teachers, teaching and school resources,
4. The so-called kindred variables, representing current characteristics of the students that should be thought of as concomitants rather than as predictors of reading achievement, and
5. The word knowledge test, as a direct index of a somewhat different sort of verbal ability.

In the discussion that follows, the separate correlations of variables chosen a priori for their possible interest will be considered first. Then the results from the regression analysis will be examined.

THE CORRELATION OF PREDICTORS WITH ACHIEVEMENT MEASURES

It seems reasonable that school characteristics would show their most marked relationships to reading achievement in Population I.

For 10-year-olds, the acquisition of basic reading skills is a fairly recent event, and instruction in reading still occupies a fairly central place in the school program. By the age of 14, skills are pretty well stabilized, and formal instruction in reading has taken a very secondary place in the school program, while at the end of secondary education, these skills are in large part taken for granted, and instruction has mostly occurred in the rather remote past. Thus, in this chapter, major attention will be directed at the 10-year-olds of Population I, less attention will be given to the 14-year-olds of Population II, and only a passing glance will be directed at the secondary school leavers of Population IV. Unfortunately, Population I is the level at which information about input variables is least adequate, so partialling out the influence of differences in input is least satisfactorily accomplished. This must be borne in mind in interpreting the results.

Table 7.1 summarizes the correlations with reading achievement in Population I for several categories of school variables. The table is arranged so that for each variable the first row displays results for the original zero-order correlations, while the second row displays the partial correlations partialling out mean rating of Father's occupation. The first section of the table deals with a group of variables that might be considered indicators of the ease with which students in a given school have access to books and reading materials. Most of the indicators are somewhat indirect. Thus, if a school has a number of librarians, it seems logical to conclude that it has a good supply of books and that students have ready access to the books. But there is always the possibility that a librarian considers it his function to protect his books from the onslaught of careless young readers, rather than to maximize the frequency with which the books are read. Thus, lack of relationship for an indicator may signify that the indicator does not well represent the basic attribute that it was designed to sample, rather than that the attribute itself is of no importance.

The chief impression that one receives from scanning the data in this first section of the table is one of inconsistency from country to country, with every variable showing both positive and negative correlations. The inconsistency may in some instances reflect genuine between-country differences. However, since the number of schools in the Population I sample ranged from 32 to 266 in different countries, much of the variation can be viewed as arising from sampling fluctuations in a series of fairly small samples.

Table 7.1. *Summary of Obtained and Partial Correlations between School and Teacher Variables and Reading Achievement. Population I*

	Range of Correlations[a]	Number Positive	Number Negative	Median Correlation
Availability of materials to be read				
1. Ease of access to public library	+.23 to −.12	10	4	.04
	+.20 to −.10	13	1	.04
2. Percent of teachers reporting class library or book corner	+.43 to −.18	7	4	.06
	+.37 to −.24	8	4	.07
3. Average size of classroom library	+.48 to −.10	11	2	.13
	+.33 to −.07	9	4	.16
4. Percent teachers reporting each child has dictionary	+.34 to −.11	10	3	.04
	+.28 to −.30	8	5	.01
5. Percent teachers reporting each student has access to own reading textbook	+.35 to −.16	6	4	.02
	+.34 to −.20	4	6	−.02
6. Amount school spends for books, stationery, etc.	+.12 to −.28	6	5	.02
	+.08 to −.33	5	7	−.02
7. Number of school librarians	+.26 to −.10	7	6	.06
	+.23 to −.13	7	5	−.03
Aspects of training and qualifications of teachers				
8. Average no. of years of full-time elem. and second. education (teachers specializing in mother tongue)	+.28 to −.20	7	6	.04
	+.41 to −.29	6	7	−.01
9. Average no. of years of full-time elem. and second. education (teachers of all subjects)	+.29 to −.19	7	7	.00
	+.28 to −.29	8	6	.02
10. Average no. of years of full-time post-secondary education (teachers of mother tongue)	+.18 to −.23	6	6	.00
	+.19 to −.35	5	8	−.05
11. Average no. of years of full-time post-secondary education (teachers of all subjects)	+.18 to −.24	6	8	−.04
	+.14 to −.35	6	8	−.04
12. Percent belonging to professional association (teachers of mother tongue)	+.26 to −.22	8	5	.10
	+.22 to −.17	9	3	.09

Table 7.1. *Population I (Cont.)*

	Range of Correlations[a]	Number Positive	Number Negative	Median Correlation
13. Percent belonging to professional association (teachers of all subjects)	+.29 to −.20 +.29 to −.15	9 9	5 3	.06 .04
14. Percent belonging to subject matter association (teachers of mother tongue)	+.26 to −.13 +.30 to −.16	9 8	3 5	.07 .05
15. Percent belonging to subject matter association (teachers of all subjects)	+.27 to −.05 +.30 to −.17	10 9	4 5	.07 .06
Availability of supporting personnel and services				
16. Number of reading specialists	+.17 to −.18 +.16 to −.18	5 5	7 7	−.02 −.01
17. Total number of ancillary personnel	+.20 to −.18 +.14 to −.17	6 8	8 6	−.03 .04
18. Availability of referral for reading problems	+.24 to −.14 +.16 to −.19	8 9	4 4	.05 .05
Evidence of individualization of instruction				
19. Student/teacher ratio	+.32 to −.35 +.32 to −.29	7 6	7 8	.00 −.02
20. Average of student-reported class size	+.29 to −.23	7	6	.01
21. Extent of practice of within-class grouping by ability (teachers of mother tongue)	+.10 to −.29 +.21 to −.31	2 5	11 6	−.09 .00
22. Extent of practice of within-class grouping by ability (teachers of all subjects)	+.12 to −.34 +.21 to −.24	2 4	12 10	−.10 −.06
23. Proportion of teachers who divide class into groups for reading instruction	+.08 to −.24 +.09 to −.33	4 4	9 9	−.08 −.07
24. Frequency of using small group work in instruction (teachers of mother tongue)	+.16 to −.22 +.16 to −.21	4 6	9 5	−.04 .00

Table 7.1. *Population I (Cont,)*

	Range of Correlations[a]	Number Positive	Number Negative	Median Correlation
25. Frequency of using small group work in instruction (teachers of all subjects)	+.15 to −.22 +.16 to −.21	4 7	9 5	−.04 .00
26. Frequency of using individual tutoring in instruction (teachers of mother tongue)	+.14 to −.21 +.19 to −.15	6 6	6 6	.00 .00
27. Frequency of using individual tutoring in instruction (teachers of all subjects)	+.14 to −.22 +.19 to −.22	7 8	7 5	.00 .02
28. Frequency of giving individual instruction in reading	+.08 to −.24 +.10 to −.21	6 5	7 8	−.04 −.04
Other teaching practices				
29. Hours spent preparing lessons (teachers of mother tongue)	+.29 to −.12	7	6	.02
30. Hours spent preparing lessons (teachers of all subjects)	+.31 to −.16	8	5	.04
31. Hours spent marking papers (teachers of mother tongue)	+.46 to −.08 +.43 to −.12	8 8	5 5	.10 .03
32. Hours spent marking papers (teachers of all subjects)	+.49 to −.06 +.47 to −.12	10 9	3 5	.10 .05
33. Percent of students reporting doing no homework	+.12 to −.30 +.23 to −.25	3 5	9 8	−.06 −.09

[a] Zero-order correlations in first row, partial correlations in second row.

One crude aproach to the question of whether a set of correlations may have arisen purely by chance is to consider the 14 countries to be independent replications and to ask what proportion of like-signed correlations would be necessary in order to be statistically significant at the 0.05 or the 0.01 level. (Some variables were available for less than the full 14 countries that tested 10-year-olds.) By this rough standard, a correlation with the same sign is required in all but two of the countries in order for the results to be significant at the 0.05 level. The only one of the first set of seven variables that meets this standard is Average size of classroom library. It emerges with a positive zero-order correlation in 11 of 13 countries, and the median of the 13 values is $+0.13$.

Of more critical concern are the partial correlations, holding average Father's occupation constant, that are summarized in the second row for each predictor. For the partial correlations, ease of access to a public library has a positive correlation in 13 of 14 countries, but the median value of the correlation is only 0.04. It is probably unreasonable to expect any of these somewhat indirect indicators to account for very much of the variation from school to school in average reading performance, but these correlations are discouragingly small, even in the few instances in which they are consistent from country to country.

Data similar to those in Table 7.1 are available also for Populations II and IV. These will be commented on in relation to the Population I data, but not presented in full. In both of the older groups, there is about the same tendency for accessibility of a public library to be related to average reading performance as is seen in Population I. However, not surprisingly, presence of a classroom book corner is no longer a favorable sign. One would anticipate that it would be at educational levels in which a student remains primarily in a home classroom that the resources of that classroom would make a difference. No other one of the first group of variables shows a consistent relationship across the three populations.

A second group of variables had to do with the training and qualifications of the teachers. None of these variables showed a consistent relationship across the set of countries, though there was a slight indication that membership in professional associations of educators or subject-matter teachers was a favorable indicator. This could perhaps be taken as one indicator of professional commitment that should be related to teaching effectiveness. The relationship was maintained in Population II, but not at the end of secondary education. A more specific inquiry was directed to finding out whether teachers had been exposed to in-service training or a formal course in the teaching of reading. There was no indication that this type of training was associated with higher average reading achievement. Correlations were slightly more often negative than positive and the median of the correlations was near to zero.

The next section deals with availability of specialized personnel to supplement the work of regular classroom teachers. Two items deal with specialized reading personnel, available either within the school or for referral. The third item summarizes the information on eight categories of supporting personnel, including counsellors, psychologists, social workers and teacher aides. Once again, the results for the 10-year-olds are inconsistent from country to country, and the median correlations are quite small. There is no indication that children read better in schools with many reading specialists even when the schools are equated for reported parental occupation. Of course, it is possible that the schools to which reading specialists tend to be assigned are those with many reading problems, and that partialling out Father's occupation does not fully compensate for this tendency. One would hesitate to conclude simply on the basis of the present results that reading specialists have no value, even though the study has failed to show an impact on reading scores.

There is a slight tendency for availability of outside referral resources for reading problems to be associated with higher reading scores of 10-year-olds. This relationship is reversed at the end of the secondary school when allowance is made for Father's occupation and Type of program. However, this is a question of median correlations of $+0.05$ and -0.07 respectively, so one should not make too much of the shift.

One criticism that has been repeatedly levelled at education over the past 50 years is that it proceeds in lock-step fashion and provides no adequate adaptation to individual differences in interest, ability or learning tempo. Teachers have been exhorted to adapt their instructional materials and procedures to the characteristics of the individual learner. Various procedures have been proposed for accomplishing this through subdividing the total class and working with small groups, through individual instruction, or through programmed and self-teaching materials. A number of questions were directed to teachers that were designed to serve as indicators of one or another aspect of potential or actual individualization of instruction.

Teachers have long maintained that one of the necessary conditions for individualization of instruction is small classes. Evidence was therefore obtained on pupil-teacher ratio, as calculated from information provided by the school administrator, as one indicator of class size, and on class size as reported by the student as another. The data from the group of 14 countries hardly support the contention that students in smaller classes will learn more. The zero-order correlations with Pupil-teacher ratio split quite evenly, with seven positive and seven negative. For student-reported Size of class the split is seven positive and six negative. The median correlation is inconsequential in both cases. Partialling out Father's occupation does not change the picture. The lack of relationship continues in Populations II and IV. Even when Father's occupation and Type of program are partialled out, there is no evidence that it is advantageous, as far as Reading Comprehension score is concerned, for the child to be in a school with small classes.

Of course, the determiners of class size are numerous and complex. Classes may be small in remote and rural schools that suffer from a variety of cultural and educational handicaps. Or assignment policies within a school may place in small classes those students having special educational problems. Thus, even though an attempt has been made to allow for certain aspects of student input, the obtained relationship—or rather, lack of relationship—cannot be considered definitive. It does suggest, however, that reducing class size will have limited impact on student performance.

One variable that did generate fairly consistent zero-order correlations with Reading Comprehension of 10-year-olds was the extent to which teachers reported within-class grouping by ability level. However, the correlation was *negative* in all but two countries. The tendency toward negative correlation became somewhat less marked when average level of Father's occupation was held constant, but the trend was still present. The negative correlation held up as strongly with the 14-year-olds as with 10-year-olds, but did not appear at the end of secondary school level. It is not known, of course, whether children achieve less well as a result of the teacher's manner of constructing within-class groups, or whether teachers who are faced with classes including a number of children with limited ability resort to formation of subgroups as a way of dealing with a difficult instructional situation. But taken at face value, the findings raise serious doubt about the effectiveness of within-class grouping as it is used by teachers to adjust to the diversity within their class.

Other indicators of individualization of instructional procedure fail to show as consistent trends of relationship to achievement, but where there are differences the correlations are more often negative than positive.

The final section of Table 7.1 reports on two or three other aspects of school practices. There is a little indication, supported also in Populations II and IV, that in schools where students more uniformly do homework, and where teachers spend more time going over that homework (and, by implication, giving students feed-back on how they have been doing), students tend to read somewhat better.

These are perhaps indicators of school and community climate, suggesting how seriously the business of schooling is being taken. In any event, these indicators provide a slight cue to reading progress.

THE REGRESSION ANALYSES

Let us turn now to the second approach based on the stepwise regression analysis. The question asked here is how much the information about school personnel, practices and procedures can add to the prediction of average reading achievement that can be made solely from knowledge of variables characterizing the input into the school. Table 7.2 shows the correlation obtainable from variables that are deemed to be "input" variables. The core of this prediction comes from the "School Handicap Score," a score based on measures of parental occupation and education, resources for reading in the home and family size (reversed). In addition, it included Type of school or Type of program, since these variables were considered to be primarily indicators of the capability of students admitted rather than an aspect of school treatment, together with variables concerning the age, grade and sex composition of the group.

Table 7.2 indicates that the most accurate prediction of achievement occurs for the 14-year-olds in Population II. For pupils in Population I, information on home and family variables is less complete, and probably less accurate. No information was sought on parental education, and father's occupation may well be less precisely reported. Furthermore, there has been less differentiation of school programs, and less assignment to programs on the basis of prior demonstration of educational competence, so that school type or program is not an effective predictor. The prediction is less good in Population IV because of the substantial degree of selection that has taken place in most countries. Since most of the less academically able are no longer in the school system, the range of talent has been reduced, and familial and socioeconomic factors that seemed to differentiate at lower levels no longer do so.

There are a few instances in which correlations of average Reading Comprehension score with input variables are quite low. Most notable is India in Population I and to a lesser extent Population II. In part, these low correlations could have arisen because of inaccuracy in the questionnaire responses produced by a group of students many of whom seemed to read even very simple material with great difficulty. This same factor may account for the low

Table 7.2. *Multiple Correlations of School Handicap Score, Age, Type of School, and Type of Program with Average Reading Comprehension for School*

Country	Population I	Population II	Population IV
Belgium (Fr)	—	—	.71
Chile	.16	.66	.73
England	.77	.90	.44
Finland	.50	.92	.48
Hungary	.46	.80	.82
India	.02	.34	.57
Iran	.53	—	.49
Israel	.81	.83	.72
Italy	.41	.78	.61
Netherlands	.63	.93	.71
New Zealand	—	.84	.51
Scotland	.84	.91	.61
Sweden	.50	.33	.72
United States	.80	.83	.72
Median	.52	.83	.66

Population I correlation for Chile. In part, these low correlations may be a genuine reflection of cultural differences, since the predictors for the School Handicap Score were selected primarily on the basis of prior experience with such predictors in the European–American setting. The low predictability of reading achievement in Sweden in Population II must be accounted for on other grounds. An examination of the variability between schools in Sweden shows it to be very small, relative to the variability among students. Thus, it appears that at this level Swedish schools are quite homogeneous, and since the differences among them are small these differences are of course inaccurately predicted.

One may ask, now, how much the prediction is improved if the most promising school variables are added to the regression equation. It will be remembered that these were the variables that survived preliminary screening and appeared to have some predictive effectiveness in at least one and usually several countries. The results are summarized in Table 7.3, which shows the multiple correlations that result after the addition of school variables, and also the increase in predictable percentage of variance resulting from the addition of these variables. (In some countries, no variables survived the screening procedure, so there was no increase in predictable variance.)

111

Table 7.3. *Multiple Correlations with Block of School Variables Added, and Added Percents of Variance Accounted for*

Country	Multiple Correlation			Added % of Variance		
	Popula-tion I	Popula-tion II	Popula-tion IV	Popula-tion I	Popula-tion II	Popula-tion IV
Belgium (Fr)	—	—	.80	—	—	14
Chile	.55	.67	.75	28	02	03
England	.77	.91	.61	00	02	18
Finland	.70	.93	.58	24	01	11
Hungary	.61	.84	.88	16	06	10
India	.44	.48	.67	19	11	11
Iran	.81	—	.76	37	—	33
Israel	.82	.81	.73	01	07	02
Italy	.52	.80	.67	11	02	07
Netherlands	.71	.95	.74	10	03	05
New Zealand	—	.92	.68	—	14	20
Scotland	.84	.91	.72	00	01	15
Sweden	.62	.58	.75	12	22	05
United States	.84	.86	.72	08	06	00
Median	.70	.85	.72	12	04	10

The increase in percentage of predictable variance ranged from zero to 37%. The smallest increase occurred in Population II, where input variables already accounted for almost 70% of the variance and left little to be predicted by other measures. The median percents of increase were 12% for Population I, 4% for Population II, and 10% for Population IV.

The above percentages look rather encouraging, at least in Populations I and IV. It thus becomes appropriate to examine the gains more closely and to ask what the variables are that lead to this improved prediction. Tables were prepared listing the variables that received weights in the regression equations, and indicating for which countries they appeared in the prediction equation. The picture was a very spotty one. This spottiness arises because many of the variables passed the screening process for admitting variables to the final regression analysis in only one or two countries, and few had an average level of correlation that led them to be included in all countries.

These variables were submitted to the computer for final regression analysis as follows:

	Popula-tion I	Popula-tion II	Popula-tion IV
Submitted in only one country	21	14	16
Submitted in 2 to 4 countries	6	3	5
Routinely submitted in all countries	1	3	3

Some variables were rejected in the computer program by the significance test that was used in deciding whether to retain a variable in the prediction equation. As a result, variables appeared in the final regression equations as follows:

	Popula-tion I	Popula-tion II	Popula-tion IV
Weighted in prediction equation for no country	10	8	1
Weighted for one country only	12	6	12
Weighted for 2 or 3 countries	4	3	4
Weighted in 4 to 7 countries	2	3	2

This analysis brings out the point that most of the school variables contributing to prediction were idiosyncratic, appearing in the prediction for only a single country, or at most two or three. In view of the size of sample of schools, which ranged from a low of about 35 in some countries in Population IV to a high of around 250 in some countries in Population I, it seems probable that a number of the singletons—those appearing in only one country—represented chance relationships that survived the somewhat relaxed screening procedure and got into the regression analysis. In any event, much of the contribution to prediction of average reading achievement by school variables that appears in the latter columns of Table 7.3 was provided by these singleton variables that emerged only in a single country.

What general statements can be made relating school variables to reading variables? This should be based upon variables that appear in the prediction equations with some consistency. In Table 7.4 the zero-order correlations and the regression weights are brought together for the four to six variables at each population level that are weighted for at least two countries. Zero-order correlations appear for each country, except for a few where data for the particular variable were missing, but weights appear only for those countries in which the variable survived the screening process and actually appeared in the regression equation.

Table 7.4. *Zero-Order Correlations and Regression Weights for School Variables as Predictors Reading Comprehension. Population I*

Country	School Environment Score		Grade in School		Teaching Specialization Index		Library in Classroom		Students Read Aloud		Teacher Urges Read Widely	
	r	Wt[a]	r	Wt	r	Wt	r	Wt	r	Wt	r	W
Chile	−.20	−.26	−.06	—	.17	.17	(−.02)	—	(.09)	—	(.06)	—
England	(.15)[b]	—	−.03	—	(.10)	—	(.19)	—	(.01)	—	(.01)	—
Finland	(−.13)	—	.26	.13	.28	.32	(.00)	—	.18	.19	.21	.28
Hungary	.24	.20	−.12	−.11	.08	—	.24	.17	−.11	—	.22	.12
India	.07	—	−.02	—	−.05	—	.14	—	.16	—	.11	—
Iran	−.53	−.29	.21	—	−.06	—	−.18	—	−.31	−.15	−.03	—
Israel	(.31)	—	.03	—	(.07)	—	(.00)	—	(−.04)	—	(.12)	—
Italy	.25	.21	.14	.11	(.11)	—	—[c]	—	—[c]	—	—[c]	—
Netherlands	(.05)	—	.04	—	—[c]	—	.45	.28	(.06)	—	(.05)	—
Scotland	(.18)	—	.19	—	(.02)	—	(−.17)	—	(−.12)	—	(.01)	—
Sweden	(.18)	—	.27	.20	(−.04)	—	(.06)	—	(.06)	—	(−.16)	—
United States	(.19)	—	.13	.16	(−.06)	—	(−.03)	—	(−.04)	—	(.11)	—

[a] When no entry shows in the "Wt" column, the variable did not survive to be weighted in the regression equation.

[b] Correlations in parentheses based on preliminary unweighted data.

[c] Data not available for this country.

The most frequently loaded variable, appearing for five countries, is Grade in school. In four countries it appears with a positive sign and in one with a negative sign. However, it could plausibly be argued that having an excess of retarded pupils in a grade below that to be expected for their age should be thought of as a reflection of below par input as much as an unfavorable school policy or treatment.

The variable appearing next most frequently in Population I is the School environment score. This is a score based upon a set of questions asked of students that deal, in general, with the degree to which the classroom is seen as authoritarian, hostile, and subject-matter centered as opposed to democratic and student-centered. A high score signifies the authoritarian end of the scale. This variable receives a weight in four countries—but in two countries the weight is positive and in two it is negative, so the effect is inconsistent from country to country. Are these differences genuine differences in the concomitants of authoritarian teaching, or is this a question of nothing more than sampling fluctuations in the data?

Table 7.4. *Population II (Cont.)*

Country	School Environment Score		Grade in School		Total Hours Homework per Week		Sex of Teacher	
	r	Wt	r	Wt	r	Wt	r	Wt
Chile	.00	—	.62	.23	.12	.09	−.19	—
England	.60	.10	.04	—	.82	—	.17	—
Finland	.63	.13	(−.44)	—	.72	—	.28	−.07
Hungary	.59	.11	(.27)	—	.62	.22	.14	—
India	.14	—	.08	—	.31	.34	.08	—
Iran	.25	—	.21	—	.42	—	.08	—
Israel	.67	.20	(.30)	—	.43	.19	−.03	—
Italy	.34	—	(.27)	—	.45	.15	−.07	−.09
Netherlands	.51	.14	(.54)	—	.74	—	−.14	.11
New Zealand	.28	.18	.56	.18	.48	.18	.00	—
Scotland	.74	.14	(.10)	—	.79	—	−.01	—
Sweden	.10	—	.19	—	.11	—	.17	.19
United States	.55	.11	.30	.17	.60	.14	−.08	−.07

Table 7.4. *Population IV (Cont.)*

Country	School Environment Score		Total Hours Homework per Week		Hours of Instruction Mother Tongue		Hours of Homework Mother Tongue	
	r	Wt	r	Wt	r	Wt	r	Wt
Belgium (Fr)	(.00)	—	.25	—	.16	—	.10	—
Chile	(.07)	—	.25	—	.11	—	−.14	—
England	(.24)	—	.03	—	−.35	—	−.36	−.29
Finland	(−.13)	—	.22	—	−.08	−.33	−.16	—
Hungary	(−.16)	—	.64	—	−.30	—	−.44	—
India	.34	.18	.22	—	.13	—	.28	.25
Iran	.23	—	.22	.21	−.26	.24	.26	—
Israel	(.22)	—	−.07	—	−.24	—	.06	—
Italy	.42	.21	.10	.11	−.20	−.13	.24	—
Netherlands	(.26)	—	−.01	—	−.10	−.22	−.05	—
New Zealand	(−.02)	—	−.01	—	−.32	−.21	−.29	—
Scotland	(.11)	—	−.03	—	−.19	—	−.41	−.32
Sweden	(.20)	—	.32	.19	−.09	—	−.14	−.17
United States	(.37)	—	.45	—	−.33	—	.00	—

The remaining variables receive weights in only two countries. An index of teaching specialization, which is a measure designed to determine the extent to which teacher assignments focus on teaching a single subject rather than all subjects, received a positive weight in Chile and Finland. Prevalence of classroom libraries or book corners was a positive indicator in Hungary and the Netherlands. Prevalence of a teaching practice of having students read aloud was positively weighted in Finland, but negatively weighted in Iran. A policy by teachers of encouraging students to read as many books as possible receives a positive weight in Finland and Hungary. Over-all, except for the frequently negative significance of retardation, there appears to be little that is consistent in the pattern of weights for this population, and one wonders whether much faith should be placed in them.

At the 14-year-old level, a glimmer of consistency appears. Two variables that seem to express the common theme of a serious, industrious approach to learning are the most frequently weighted. One is the School environment score mentioned in relation to Population I, while the other is the reported Number of hours homework per week. One or both of these variables receives a positive weight in 11 of 13 countries for which the regression analyses were carried out, and the zero-order correlations of these variables with Reading Comprehension score are generally substantial. At this level, schools in most countries are quite differentiated in student input and type of program, and these two indicators of grim effort tend to be substantially correlated with the input variables. However, they do generally seem to add a little something further to prediction, so that among those schools of a given caliber of input, the ones that demand the most effort seem to produce the best readers.

The remaining variables seem spotty and inconsistent. A predominance of male teachers is a favorable indicator in Finland and Italy, a predominance of female teachers in the Netherlands and Sweden. A predominance of pupils of higher grade level receives a positive weight in Chile, New Zealand and the United States.

We turn finally to Population IV, the group at the end of secondary education. The results at this level seem rather uneven. In five countries there is a weight for Hours devoted to the study of mother tongue, but in four of the five the weight is negative, i.e., more hours is associated with lower Reading Comprehension score. In four other countries Hours of homework in mother tongue is weighted, with three of the four weights being negative. In three countries Total hours of homework receives a positive regression weight. School environment score receives a positive weight in two countries. One can still see in this set of weights some evidence of positive value attached to serious effort (homework, school environment score). It has also been suggested that the poorer schools with weaker pupils are likely to offer fewer subjects, and that as a consequence more time is devoted to mother tongue in these schools. Perhaps one should not expect school practices at the end of secondary school to have any impact on reading ability, since reading skills were probably established much earlier in the academic careers of the students.

What can one say in general about the impact of school variables upon Reading Comprehension as appraised in this study? Little that is positive or general. When variables are selected because they might reasonably show relationships, they fail to do so with any consistency. When variables are picked empirically because they add to prediction, the variables are largely peculiar to one or two countries and/or are inconsistent in their weighting, or difficult to rationalize. It must be admitted that little emerges that helps to understand what a school can do to foster better achievement in its students.

In addition to home and school variables that might be considered predictors of achievement, information was obtained on a number of variables that might be considered concomitants of achievement. These are largely variables describing the present state or future plans of a student or of the students in a particular school. This group includes variables such as those concerned with the student's reported liking for school, his amount of free time reading, his preference for different types of reading, and his future educational and vocational plans. These have been spoken of in the project as "kindred" variables since they are contemporaneous with the measure of reading ability but are neither clearly cause nor effect of reading achievement. These kindred variables have received some discussion in Chapter 6 in connection with the between-student differences in reading ability. They also emerge in the between-school analyses.

The kindred variables were introduced into the regression equations in a block *following* the school variables and the home background variables. In spite of being added late in the sequence of variables, there were a number of them that appeared with appreciable weights for a number of the countries. The zero-order correlations and regression weights for Populations I, II and IV are shown in Table 7.5.

Table 7.5. *Zero-Order Correlations and Regression Weights for "Kindred" or Concomitant Variables as Predictors of Reading Comprehension. Population I*

Country	Liking for School		School Motivation to do Well		Hours TV per Day		Hours Reading for Pleasure	
	r	Wt	r	Wt	r	Wt	r	Wt
Chile	.47	.24	.42	.34	−.07	—	.10	—
England	.00	−.19	.40	.18	−.36	−.08	.46	.12
Finland	.11	−.21	.40	.40	−.14	−.22	.14	.11
Hungary	−.07	—	.00	—	.11	—	.42	.22
India	.56	.47	.37	—	−.19	—	.02	—
Iran	.52	.38	.46	—	.01	—	−.01	−.14
Israel	.03	—	.45	.13	−.38	−.19	.47	—
Italy	.19	.15	.44	.19	.10	.09	.36	.17
Netherlands	.16	.15	.10	—	−.35	−.20	.55	.29
Scotland	.01	—	.28	—	−.47	−.11	.70	.20
Sweden	.13	—	.25	—	−.20	−.17	.37	—
United States	−.07	−.11	.62	.23	−.37	−.09	.28	—

In Population I, the variable that was most consistent in its correlations and in receiving a positive weight was the School motivation score. This was based on the students' answers to such questions as:

It is important for you to do well in school?

Do you work hard most of the time?

Do you hope eventually to go to college (the university)?

With one exception, the average Motivation score showed a positive correlation with average Reading Comprehension, and in six of 12 countries it received a positive regression weight.

Reported Liking for school was based on items such as:

The most enjoyable part of my life is the time I spend in school.

I generally dislike my school work.

There are many school subjects I don't like.

The relation of average Liking for school to average Reading Comprehension score was far from consistent across countries. In three of 12 countries the correlation was zero or negative, in many the correlation had a low positive value. In the three developing countries, however (where general level of reading was quite low), correlation between expressed Liking for school and reading achievement was quite high, and the variable received a substantial positive weight in the regression equation.

Table 7.5. *Population II* (*Cont.*)

Country	Parental Interest Index r	Wt	Reading Preference Index r	Wt	Frequency Movies r	Wt	Hours Reading for Pleasure r	Wt	Expected Education and Occupation r	Wt
Chile	.36	—	.45	—	.15	−.18	.47	.14	.46	—
England	.35	−.11	.77	.14	−.27	−.05	.67	—	.79	—
Finland	.46	−.12	.71	.16	.34	−.12	.29	—	.86	—
Hungary	.06	—	.56	.14	.02	—	.65	.08	.79	.29
India	−.23	−.14	.50	.40	−.16	—	−.01	—	.14	—
Israel	−.13	−.17	.54	.24	−.05	−.07	.30	—	.47	—
Italy	.07	−.16	.36	.09	−.14	—	.29	—	.44	.08
Netherlands	.62	.12	.73	—	−.32	—	.42	—	.87	—
New Zealand	.49	—	.43	.09	−.16	—	.42	—	.54	—
Scotland	.52	—	.71	.18	−.30	−.12	.75	—	.78	.21
Sweden	.16	—	.45	.31	−.24	−.19	.12	—	.28	—
United States	.05	−.29	.57	—	.01	—	.59	.23	.52	—

Table 7.5. *Population IV* (*Cont.*)

Country	Parents Correct Speech and Writing r	Wt	Expected Education and Occupation r	Wt	Reading Preference Index r	Wt	Place of Science in the World r	Wt
Belgium (Fr)	−.05	—	.60	—	—[a]	—	—[a]	—
Chile	.07	−.19	.54	—	—[a]	—	.45	.21
England	.14	—	−.08	−.19	.35	.33	.16	.33
Finland	−.09	−.16	.22	—	.11	—	.20	—
Hungary	−.19	−.17	.72	—	—[a]	—	.32	—
India	−.13	−.14	.06	—	.63	.35	.39	.25
Iran	.04	—	.27	—	.53	—	−.12	—
Israel	.22	—	.35	.15	—[a]	—	—[a]	—
Italy	−.09	−.24	.31	—	.50	.14	.32	.18
Netherlands	.38	.23	.14	—	—[a]	—	.48	—
New Zealand	−.24	−.21	.09	—	(.39)[b]	—	.07	—
Scotland	−.20	—	.49	.32	.16	—	.14	—
Sweden	−.26	−.11	.46	.21	.25	.15	.07	—
United States	.04	—	.51	—	.25	—	.06	—

[a] Variable not analyzed for this country.
[b] Correlations in parentheses based on original unweighted data.

Reported Hours of reading for pleasure was rather generally positively correlated with reading achievement, and this variable received a positive regression weight in six of 12 countries and a negative weight in one. By contrast, Time spent watching television was typically slightly negatively correlated with achievement, receiving a modest negative loading in seven of the 12 countries and a positive loading in only one. These results support the image of the high achiever as a child who spends at least some time reading and who devotes correspondingly less time to the visual displays of television.

Amount of reading for pleasure continues to show almost universally positive relationships to Reading Comprehension score in Population II, though the variable has a loading (positive) in the regression equation for only three countries. In Population II, much of the possible prediction of reading is already exhausted by input variables, so further information on free reading makes little new contribution.

Among the 14-year-olds, movie attendance appears to function in a manner analogous to TV viewing for 10-year-olds. Correlations of Reading Comprehension score with Frequency of movie attendance are generally negative, and the variable receives a negative weight in six regression equations.

At the upper ages a weighted index based on amount and type of reading was developed. The weighting of different categories of books and magazines and of different sections of the daily paper was based on preliminary data from between-student analyses of the types that were preferred by more competent readers. Weighting was carried out country by country so as to maximize approximately the correlation for that country. As a consequence, it is hardly surprising that the correlations are positive and generally substantial, and that the variable receives a positive weight in the regression equation for many countries.

A further variable that almost always shows a positive correlation with Reading Comprehension concerns the students' Expected education and Expected occupation. An index was developed based on a composite of these two expectations. This showed positive correlations in all but one instance and occasionally quite high correlations with achievement, but its correlations with home background and school type were also high. Hence regression weights for this variable were generally small, though positive, and it made relatively little independent contribution to the predictions.

At the Population IV level an additional variable that was examined was a scale of attitude towards the place of science in the world. Rather generally, those schools in which the students saw science as making important contributions to human living were ones in which the reading performance was above average. However, the relationships were generally small, and in some countries they reflected between-school differences in input. In only four countries was this variable weighted in the regression.

Finally, in Populations II and IV, a variable was analyzed based on students' reports that their parents were interested in and helped with school work (Population II), or that parents corrected the student's speech and writing (Population IV). The Parental interest and help variables had generally positive zero-order correlations in Population II, but due to the relationship of these variables to student input and other prior variables, the regression weights were negative in six of seven cases. Thus, other things being equal as it were, the school where many parents pitch in to help their children is likely to be a school where many children need help, and one in which achievement is correspondingly below par. The same thing can, in general, be said of the Population IV variables, Parents correct speech and writing. In the case of these two variables, it is a little uncertain as to whether they should be considered "kindred" or "input" variables.

As one looks over the results on the kindred variables, and compares them with results for the school variables, one receives an impression of rather more consistency and substance. There is more agreement across countries, and a rather more substantial contribution to prediction of Reading Comprehension score. This is hardly surprising, since the variables are ones that characterize individuals *directly* and that have been chosen because they seem relevant to achievement. Together with the measures of home background and school type, they seem to account for most of the variation from one school to another just as they account for most of the variation from one individual to another.

SUMMARY

As one views the results on school factors related to reading achievement it is hard not to feel somewhat disappointed and let down. There is so little that provides a basis for any positive or constructive action on the part of teachers or administrators. There is so little consistent identification of school factors that make a difference. Is this because the significant educational factors are not adequately represented in the evidence that was gathered by questionnaires completed by students, teachers and administrators? Is it because the important school influences on reading are ones that operate before even the level of Population I, in the first year or two of school experience? Is it because the important school influences are mediated by specific teachers, and the relevant teacher need not be the present one or be identified in the Teacher Questionnaires completed by a sample of teachers currently in the school? Or is it true that when it comes to *comprehension*, the basic ability of the child is modified more by a wide range of home and community factors than by variations in schooling? On issues such as these the present study provides more questions than answers.

Chapter 8

Factors Associated with Between-Country Differences in Reading Achievement

It is of some interest to examine the differences in reading achievement between countries, and to look for the differences in characteristics of the national culture, language or educational system that may account for the differences. Since the number of countries for which data are available is at most 15, and since countries differ in a great number of ways, it is hardly possible to establish which of the many differences are the ones that are important in accounting for differences in achievement. Any interpretation of observed relationships must be highly tentative.

Several subscores were obtained for the Reading Comprehension test, and it will be of some interest to examine the pattern of relative strength and weakness of the subscores, as well as on the Reading speed test, and perhaps the test of word knowledge.

The basic data for the participating countries are shown in Table 8.1 for the samples of 10-year-olds, in Table 8.2 for the samples of 14-year-olds, and in Table 8.3 for the samples tested in the final year of secondary school. Means and standard deviations are shown for total Reading Comprehension test and for each of the subtests, for Reading speed (except for Population IV), and for Word knowledge.

The pattern of achievement within a country cannot be readily determined from the above tables, since the different tests and subtests have quite different means, standard deviations, and reliability coefficients. In an effort to make the results more directly comparable for the different tests and subtests, all national means were converted into a type of standard score, using the following procedures:

1. The standard deviation of true scores was estimated for each measure in each population, using the formula

$$\hat{\sigma}_{x_\infty} = \bar{S}_x \sqrt{\bar{r}_{xx'}}$$

123

Table 8.1. *Means and Standard Deviations by Country for Reading and Word Knowledge Tests. Population I*

| | Reading Comprehension | | | | | | | | | | Reading Speed | | | | Word Knowledge | |
| | Total | | Subscore A | | Subscore C | | Subscore D | | Subscore E | | No. Attempted | | Error Score | | | |
Country	Mean	SD	Mean	SD	Mean	SD	Mean	SD	Mean	SD	Mean	SD	Mean	SD	Mean	SD
Belgium (Fl)	17.5	9.2	0.2	1.1	7.5	3.4	5.5	4.0	1.0	1.6	27.2	8.9	0.7	1.2	21.9	9.3
Belgium (Fr)	17.9	9.3	0.5	1.1	7.5	3.6	4.9	3.8	1.8	1.6	27.6	9.6	0.8	1.3	22.1	9.9
Chile	9.1	9.3	0.3	1.0	3.8	4.1	2.8	3.5	0.7	1.5	28.8	11.8	2.3	2.0	15.4	11.8
England	18.5	11.6	0.8	1.2	7.2	4.4	5.9	4.6	1.5	1.6	25.1	8.9	0.8	1.4	17.6	11.4
Finland	19.4	10.8	0.4	1.1	7.8	4.0	6.1	4.2	1.7	1.8	25.4	8.2	1.0	1.6	19.2	8.8
Hungary	14.0	9.8	0.7	1.2	5.6	3.9	4.3	3.6	1.0	1.6	22.7	9.2	1.8	1.8	22.4	12.6
India	8.5	9.4	0.2	1.0	4.3	3.9	2.0	3.5	0.6	1.4	37.2	7.4	3.2	2.3	12.5	10.7
Iran	3.7	6.9	0.2	1.0	1.8	3.3	1.0	2.7	0.1	1.2	23.4	12.5	4.7	2.2	11.7	10.8
Israel	13.8	11.0	0.5	1.1	5.7	4.3	4.5	4.2	0.8	1.5	22.8	10.5	1.6	1.6	12.8	10.3
Italy	19.9	8.8	1.1	1.1	7.4	3.2	6.6	3.7	0.9	1.2	32.9	7.5	1.0	1.2	28.6	10.2
Netherlands	17.7	9.5	0.6	1.2	7.1	3.8	5.9	4.0	0.7	1.4	25.7	8.2	0.8	1.2	17.5	9.0
Scotland	18.4	11.1	0.8	1.2	7.2	4.3	5.8	4.4	1.4	1.6	24.6	8.4	0.9	1.4	15.7	11.2
Sweden	21.5	10.5	0.6	1.1	8.4	4.0	7.2	4.4	1.6	1.6	23.9	7.4	0.6	1.4	14.2	7.5
United States	16.8	11.6	1.0	1.2	6.3	4.3	4.9	4.6	1.7	1.7	24.7	8.6	1.0	1.5	17.4	11.2
Median	17.6	9.6	0.6	1.1	7.2	4.0	5.2	4.0	1.0	1.6	25.2	8.8	1.0	1.4	17.4	10.5

Table 8.2. *Means and Standard Deviations by Country for Reading and Word Knowledge Tests. Population II*

| Country | Reading Comprehension | | | | | | | | | | Reading Speed | | | | Word Knowledge | |
| | Total | | Subscore B | | Subscore C | | Subscore D | | Subscore E | | No. Attempted | | Error Score | | | |
	Mean	SD	Mean	SD	Mean	SD	Mean	SD	Mean	SD	Mean	SD	Mean	SD	Mean	SD
Belgium (Fl)	24.6	9.7	0.6	1.3	4.6	2.0	13.0	5.2	1.7	1.7	33.1	7.2	0.3	0.7	26.8	8.7
Belgium (Fr)	27.2	8.7	1.2	1.4	5.2	1.8	13.0	4.8	2.5	1.5	34.4	6.5	0.2	0.5	23.8	8.7
Chile	14.1	11.1	0.2	1.2	2.7	2.5	6.9	6.0	1.3	1.7	30.0	9.0	1.4	1.6	13.3	10.8
England	25.3	11.9	0.6	1.3	4.4	2.2	13.0	6.6	2.5	1.7	32.6	7.9	0.3	0.8	15.4	9.7
Finland	27.1	10.9	1.3	1.6	4.6	2.1	13.5	5.7	2.9	1.7	30.7	6.5	0.7	1.6	16.8	9.6
Hungary	25.5	9.9	1.2	1.6	4.2	2.1	12.9	5.0	2.2	1.8	29.4	7.8	0.7	1.0	28.3	10.3
India	5.2	7.2	0.1	1.2	1.7	2.0	1.1	3.9	0.5	1.4	36.3	7.5	2.9	2.2	6.7	9.3
Iran	7.8	6.7	0.2	1.2	1.9	1.8	2.6	3.9	1.2	1.5	24.4	10.5	1.8	1.5	19.6	9.6
Israel	22.6	12.8	1.2	1.5	3.6	2.4	11.6	7.0	1.9	1.7	26.6	9.1	0.8	1.0	17.7	11.0
Italy	27.9	9.3	1.3	1.5	4.6	1.9	14.3	5.0	2.5	1.5	34.1	6.8	0.8	1.3	26.1	8.6
Netherlands	25.2	10.2	0.8	1.4	4.8	2.0	13.1	5.1	2.0	1.8	32.1	6.7	0.4	0.8	18.7	8.7
New Zealand	29.3	11.0	0.9	1.4	5.0	1.9	14.7	6.1	3.0	1.6	31.0	7.6	0.3	0.8	16.8	9.4
Scotland	27.0	11.5	0.7	1.3	4.8	2.0	13.8	6.4	2.6	1.7	33.1	7.0	0.3	0.8	15.9	9.9
Sweden	25.6	10.8	0.5	1.4	4.8	2.0	13.0	5.6	2.6	2.0	34.2	6.0	0.2	0.6	13.6	8.4
United States	27.3	11.6	1.0	1.4	4.8	1.9	13.2	6.2	2.8	1.9	32.4	7.2	0.3	0.8	16.8	8.8
Median	25.5	10.8	0.8	1.4	4.6	2.0	13.0	5.6	2.5	1.7	32.4	7.2	0.4	0.8	16.8	9.4

Table 8.3. *Means and Standard Deviations by Country for Reading and Word Knowledge Tests. Population IV*

Country	Reading Comprehension Total Mean	SD	Subscore B Mean	SD	Subscore C Mean	SD	Subscore D Mean	SD	Subscore E Mean	SD	Word Knowledge Mean	SD
Belgium (Fl)	25.0	9.3	2.7	1.7	5.9	2.2	5.6	3.6	2.8	1.7	26.8	6.1
Belgium (Fr)	27.6	9.2	3.4	1.5	5.6	2.2	7.9	3.8	3.0	1.6	32.0	6.8
Chile	16.0	8.8	1.9	1.7	3.7	2.4	4.7	3.4	2.4	1.6	23.1	9.5
England	33.6	9.0	3.4	1.5	7.2	1.8	10.1	3.7	3.5	1.6	24.8	7.4
Finland	30.0	7.5	3.2	1.5	6.5	1.9	8.9	3.2	3.8	1.4	15.9	6.6
Hungary	23.8	8.9	2.6	1.7	5.9	2.2	6.9	3.5	2.5	1.6	33.9	5.6
India	3.5	5.8	0.6	1.5	1.3	2.1	1.2	2.6	0.3	1.4	9.1	8.3
Iran	4.4	6.0	0.3	1.4	1.3	2.1	1.1	2.5	0.3	1.4	23.4	8.2
Israel	25.2	10.8	2.6	1.8	5.7	2.4	7.6	4.1	2.3	1.6	18.1	7.7
Italy	23.9	10.2	2.6	1.9	5.1	2.5	6.4	3.7	2.8	1.6	33.1	5.8
Netherlands	31.2	7.0	2.6	1.4	5.8	1.7	9.6	3.3	3.0	1.4	28.2	6.4
New Zealand	35.4	8.1	3.4	1.5	7.2	1.8	10.9	3.4	3.6	1.4	24.7	8.2
Scotland	34.4	8.2	3.3	1.4	7.5	1.6	10.4	3.5	3.5	1.5	24.5	7.6
Sweden	26.8	9.3	2.3	1.7	6.0	2.0	8.1	3.7	3.1	1.6	25.0	7.4
United States	21.8	12.0	2.1	1.8	5.0	2.8	5.8	4.3	3.1	1.9	13.7	9.7
Median	25.2	8.9	2.6	1.5	5.8	2.1	7.6	3.5	3.0	1.6	24.7	7.4

where $\hat{\bar{\sigma}}_{x_\infty}$ = estimated true score standard deviation

$\bar{S}_x$ = median observed sample standard deviation

$\bar{r}_{xx'}$ = median reliability coefficient for the measure.

2. A general cross-national average was estimated, using as an estimate the median of the within-country means. (The median was chosen as a preferred measure of central tendency because it would be less influenced than the mean by extreme values in one or two countries.)

3. For each country the difference between its mean and the general average was divided by the median within-country standard deviation of true scores found in step (1), and multiplied by 10. This somewhat elaborate procedure was adopted in order to take account not only of the differences in mean and standard deviation but also of the differences in reliability of the various tests and subtests.

The converted scores resulting from this transformation are shown

Table 8.4. *National Means for Reading Tests and Subtests Expressed in Uniform Standard Score Units. Population I*

| Country | Reading Comprehension | | | | | Reading Speed | Word Knowledge |
	Total	Type A	Type C	Type D	Type E		
Belgium (Fl)	0	− 9	1	1	0	3	5
Belgium (Fr)	0	− 2	1	− 1	10	3	5
Chile	− 10	− 7	− 10	− 8	− 4	5	− 2
England	1	4	0	2	6	0	0
Finland	2	− 4	2	3	8	0	2
Hungary	− 4	2	− 5	− 3	0	− 3	5
India	− 11	− 9	− 8	− 10	− 5	16	− 5
Iran	− 16	− 9	− 15	− 13	− 11	− 2	− 6
Israel	− 4	− 2	− 4	− 2	− 2	− 3	− 5
Italy	3	11	1	4	− 1	10	12
Netherlands	0	0	0	2	− 4	1	0
Scotland	1	4	0	2	5	− 1	− 2
Sweden	5	0	3	6	7	− 2	− 3
United States	− 1	9	− 3	− 1	8	− 1	0

Table 8.5. *National Means for Reading Tests and Subtests Expressed in Uniform Standard Score Units. Population II*

| Country | Reading Comprehension | | | | | Reading Speed | Word Knowledge |
	Total	Type B	Type C	Type D	Type E		
Belgium (Fl)	− 1	− 2	0	0	− 9	1	12
Belgium (Fr)	2	4	4	0	0	3	8
Chile	− 12	− 7	− 13	− 13	− 13	− 4	− 4
England	0	− 2	− 1	0	0	0	− 2
Finland	2	5	0	1	4	− 3	0
Hungary	0	4	− 3	0	− 3	− 5	14
India	− 21	− 8	− 19	− 24	− 22	− 4	− 13
Iran	− 18	− 7	− 18	− 21	− 14	− 12	3
Israel	− 3	4	− 7	− 3	− 7	− 9	1
Italy	3	5	0	3	0	3	11
Netherlands	0	0	0	0	− 6	0	2
New Zealand	4	1	3	3	6	− 2	0
Scotland	2	− 1	1	2	1	1	− 1
Sweden	0	− 3	1	0	1	3	− 4
United States	2	2	1	0	3	0	0

Table 8.6. *National Means for Reading Tests and Subtests Expressed in Uniform Standard Score Units. Population IV*

| Country | Reading Comprehension | | | | | Word Knowledge |
	Total	Type B	Type C	Type D	Type E	
Belgium (Fl)	− 1	1	1	− 7	− 2	3
Belgium (Fr)	2	0	− 1	2	0	11
Chile	− 13	− 9	− 15	− 10	− 5	− 3
England	10	10	10	10	4	0
Finland	6	8	5	6	6	− 14
Hungary	− 3	0	1	− 2	− 4	14
India	− 30	− 26	− 32	− 23	− 21	− 24
Iran	− 28	− 30	− 32	− 23	− 21	− 2
Israel	0	0	0	0	− 6	− 10
Italy	− 3	0	− 5	− 4	− 2	12
Netherlands	7	0	0	8	0	5
New Zealand	13	10	10	13	5	0
Scotland	11	9	12	11	4	0
Sweden	1	− 4	1	3	1	0
United States	− 5	− 7	− 6	− 6	1	− 17

in Table 8.4 for Population I, Table 8.5 for Population II, and Table 8.6 for Population IV. These tables make it possible to see directly the level and patterning of achievement in different countries.

BETWEEN-COUNTRY DIFFERENCES IN LEVEL

Examination of the values in any specific column of Tables 8.4, 8.5 and 8.6 provides information on between-country differences on the specific test or subtest represented by that column. Chief interest centers on the columns representing total scores, especially the total score for Reading Comprehension.

Total score for Reading Comprehension, expressed in standard score units in which one point equals one tenth of a standard deviation, appear in the first column of Tables 8.4, 8.5 and 8.6. The results show in general that three of the countries to which the designation "developing country" might be applied are consistently well below the remaining countries at each of the population levels. The difference appears to be about one to one and a half standard deviations in Population I, from one to two standard deviations in

Population II, and from one and a third to three standard deviations in Population IV. The variation among the remaining 12 countries is relatively small, and somewhat inconsistent from age level to age level. Among the 10-year-olds, the country that showed the highest level of Reading Comprehension was Sweden, where the mean is about one half of a standard deviation above the median of means. This is followed by Italy with a plus deviation of three tenths of a standard deviation. Two countries doing somewhat less than average at this level are Hungary and Israel, each of which falls four tenths of a standard deviation below the general group average. In Population II, the differences among the remaining countries continue to be fairly modest. Highest level of performance appears in New Zealand and Italy, and slightly below average performance is once again found in Israel. As will be seen presently, Israel has a very large standard deviation of reading scores, and the somewhat lowered average and very great variability in that country are probably to be understood in terms of the heterogeneity of the immigrant population. The combination of immigration from Western Europe on the one hand and from the nearby Asiatic countries on the other has produced a very mixed population with quite varied cultural and educational histories, and this is presumably what has generated the results found here. In Population IV, the differences between the countries with the highest level of reading performance and those with the lowest are substantially greater than at the earlier levels. This is probably a natural occurrence, reflecting not only the cumulative effects of any educational experience but also the fairly wide range in selectivity operating in the different national programs. The highest level of reading achievement at this level is found in England, New Zealand and Scotland. In these countries, the estimates of proportion of students still in school in the final year of secondary education and constituting the target population are respectively 20 %, 13 %, and 17 %. The lowest country, apart from the three developing countries, is now the United States, and this corresponds to a retention in the final year of secondary education estimated to be 75 %. For the 12 developed countries, the rank-order correlation between the proportion of the age group excluded from the target population and average Reading Comprehension score is 0.63. Thus it appears that some substantial part of the difference in score among the developed countries is to be accounted for by difference in retentivity. However, it is not possible to make a sound adjustment for differences in retentivity unless one can assess how much overlap in test performance there would be between those who remained in the target population and those who dropped out.

The next four columns in Tables 8.4, 8.5 and 8.6 show standard scores for subtypes of reading skills. These columns must be used with considerable caution because the number of items in certain of the categories was very small and the reliabilities on the tests were correspondingly low. Earlier (Chapter 4), these reliabilities were examined in relation to the intercorrelations of the subscores, and it was concluded that subscore differences represented to a very substantial degree nothing but measurement error. It will suffice to review these results rather briefly, commenting only on findings that are based upon data of some substance. In Population I, type A and type E reading items (referring respectively to knowledge of word meanings in context and to ability to infer the author's mood or purpose from the passage) were each based upon only three items and hardly merit consideration. The word knowledge items appear to be easier in Hungary, Iran, Italy, and the United States. In three of the countries (Hungary, India and Iran) performance on the Word knowledge test was also relatively good, so it is possible that the vocabulary is either better known or simpler in Hungarian, Hindi and Persian than it is in English. Countries doing relatively poorly were Flemish-speaking Belgium, Finland and Sweden. Sweden also did relatively poorly on the Word knowledge test, so it is possible that the basic vocabulary presents a little more of a difficulty in Sweden than it does collectively across the set of countries. Reading of type E was performed better than the average for all types of reading in French-speaking Belgium, Chile, England, Finland, India, Iran, and the United States. Four of these countries also did relatively well on this type of reading in Population II, but none of them were especially outstanding in Population IV. At the moment there seems to be no good rationale for why the performance was effective on these three items at this level, and one must suspect that it was an idiosyncrasy of the formulation in the specific languages of the participating countries. In Population I, the bulk of the reading items were classified in categories C and D. These are defined respectively as ability to answer questions that are specifically answered in the passage and ability to draw inferences from the passage about its contents. It was hoped that perhaps this classification might provide some cues as to the type of reading skills that were being developed in the several countries. However, in neither Population I nor Population II were there substantial differences between these two types of reading for any country. Those countries that did well in one did well in the other, and vice versa. The difference was rarely more than two tenths of a standard deviation. Furthermore, differences that were found tended not to be consistent from one population level to the next.

In Population II, type B reading items (ability to follow the organization of the passage and to identify antecedents and references in it) appear for the first time. There are only a few items of this type, and the fact that Chile, India, Iran, and Israel do relatively better on these than they do on the more frequent items of fact (C) and inference (D) probably should not receive much weight. The only other differences in Population II are a below average performance by Flemish-speaking Belgium and the Netherlands on the type E items, on which they fall below their performance on the other types of items on the test.

In Population IV, the evidences of patterning are again rather limited. The test seemed to contain a preponderance on inference items (type D), and somewhat surprisingly the developing countries did better on these items than they did on relatively direct statements of fact. Most of the patterning at Population IV appears in respect to the type E items (author's purpose). However, this may be merely a reflection of the fact that these items are not very numerous in the test, and that correspondingly they are not as highly related to the bulk of the test as are items of other types. Thus, the spread of standard scores appears to be less for these items, and the countries that do well do not do quite as well on them, whereas the countries that do poorly in general do less poorly on these. The spread between countries in these somewhat more indirect, aesthetic, and inferential types of items seems to be less than in the more straightforward measures of literal comprehension of the cognitive message of the passage.

The Word knowledge test is of limited interest as far as cross-national, and especially cross-language comparisons are concerned. Though a good deal of effort was devoted to producing translations of the English-language items that had a difficulty comparable to the originals, and to selecting from those tried out the ones that showed a consistent difficulty level across languages, the attempt was only partially successful. As a result, the equivalence of the test across languages is more seriously in question than is the case for reading of connected prose. However, some consideration of the results is in order.

Examination of the last column of Table 8.4 shows results for vocabulary in Population I not greatly different from those for comprehension. The developed countries show modest differences, even across languages, but the economically less developed countries fall behind. However, at the higher educational levels, the pattern changes fairly radically. This is seen most clearly in Population IV, where non-English-speaking European countries reach the highest scores, and the English-speaking countries lag well behind. It seems likely that the difference arose from translation problems with the test. As developmental work on the test was proceeding, preparation of synonym–antonym items that were of equivalent difficulty to their English originals seemed to present no great problems at the lower and intermediate difficulty levels. However, items specially designed to tap the limits of vocabulary in English tended to lose the element of special difficulty when translated. An example is the item

pessimistic – sanguine

This is an extremely difficult item for English-speaking secondary school students. However, the semantically equivalent item

pessimistic – optimistic

would be quite easy. One suspects that (for lack of an appropriate direct translation of "sanguine") translations tended to approximate the much easier paraphrase, rather than the actual test item.

At the Population I level, there was essentially no consistency as between countries in rank for scores of comprehension and speed. In particular, Sweden, which was highest in Reading Comprehension score, tied for 11th in 14 for speed, while India, which was 13th in comprehension was first in average speed score and Chile, which was 12th in comprehension was third in speed. One suspects that in the two latter countries the paragraphs were only nominally "read" and that the process involved little or no comprehension of what had passed before the eyes. Evidence for this is found in the very high proportion of errors made by students in these countries in responding to even the simple items of the speed of reading exercise.

In Population II the correspondence between reading speed and comprehension is more substantial, and is represented by a rank-difference correlation across countries of $+0.53$. India still makes out a good deal better on the speed than on the comprehension test, but the gross discrepancy found in Population I is no longer present. In general, differences between countries in speed score are less then they are in comprehension score where the developing countries fall far behind the others.

LEVEL OF READING MASTERY

All of the discussion so far has been in terms of scores and of relative performance in different countries. One should perhaps also try to convey some impression of the absolute standard of accomplishment that the scores attained by the students in different countries represent. This is not easy to do. However, some impression can be obtained if one examines one or more of the actual passages, together with the questions based upon it, and relates the test items to the percent of students in each country getting them wrong. Below we present one of the easier passages in the test for each group—10-year-olds, 14-year-olds, and end of secondary school. The passages and questions are followed by a tabulation (Tables 8.7, 8.8 and 8.9) showing the percent *failing* the item in each country. The tabulations are then followed by some comments.

Population I

Passage and Items

One of the most interesting birds I have seen is the Indian Tailor Bird. It is a small olive green bird that doesn't look at all unusual, yet it has a most unusual way of making its nest. The birds work together in pairs. First they find a leaf, the right size, and make holes along the edges with their beaks. Through these holes they thread grass. One bird pushes the thread from the outside, while the other bird sits in the nest and pushes it back until the edges of the leaf are sewn together to make a kind of bag, still hanging on the tree, in which the Tailor Bird lays its eggs.

1. What does the Tailor Bird use in place of thread?
   A. Grass
   B. String
   C. Spider web
   D. Thorns

2. The Tailor Birds are interesting because they
   A. are small and olive green in color.
   B. live in pairs.
   C. make their nests in a special way.
   D. fly very fast.

3. The Tailor Bird got that name because it
A. is a small bird.
B. looks unusual.
C. can sew.
D. has a beak shaped like a needle.

5. The person who wrote about Tailor Birds was trying to
A. give you some new information.
B. tell you a story.
C. get you to share his feelings.
D. keep you guessing on how the story will come out.

4. The Tailor Birds make their nests
A. from leaves.
B. in a hole in a tree.
C. in the tall grass.
D. with a lining of grass.

Table 8.7. *Percent Failing. Population I*

Country	Item 1	Item 2	Item 3	Item 4	Item 5
Belgium (Fl)	5	44	53	40	43
Belgium (Fr)	12	27	52	27	30
Chile	16	48	53	41	60
England	10	37	37	27	37
Finland	16	36	26	22	31
Hungary	8	40	32	39	48
India	16	66	58	54	61
Iran	56	75	65	56	66
Israel	12	49	42	46	56
Italy	8	32	80	23	32
Netherlands	8	28	48	41	38
Scotland	11	38	35	30	38
Sweden	10	35	39	27	36
United States	13	35	46	38	33

Clearly, the little paragraph shown here is at a level that presents difficulty to a substantial fraction of 10-year-olds in every country. Considering all 14 countries and all five items, the typical failure percentage runs between 35% and 40% (Table 8.7). The median percentage goes as low as 26% in Finland, but is 48% in Chile, 58% in India and 65% in Iran. When one considers that random marking would be expected to give only 75% of error on these four-choice items, it becomes clear that even this passages is pushing the limit of competence of most 10-year-olds in these three countries.

A further indication of the base level of competence in the developing countries is provided by error rate on the first nine items of the test of reading speed. These are items such as:

"Peter has a little dog. The dog is black with a white spot on his back and one white leg. The color of Peter's dog is mostly

       black   brown   gray"

The percentage of wrong answers on items such as this is as follows:

Country	10-year-olds	14-years-olds
Belgium (Fl)	8	3
Belgium (Fr)	9	2
Chile	26	16
England	9	4
Finland	11	8
Hungary	20	8
India	36	33
Iran	52	20
Israel	17	9
Italy	11	9
Netherlands	8	4
New Zealand	—	4
Scotland	10	3
Sweden	7	2
United States	11	4

In the European countries, a typical error rate on these items is about 10% for 10-year-olds and 4% for 14-year-olds. With these values, one must contrast percentages of 26, 36 and 52 for 10-year-olds of the developing countries (Chile, India and Iran) and 16%, 33% and 20% for the 14-year-olds. Admittedly, this material was given as a speed test. But it was also given as a reading test! If a substantial proportion of the students in a school system have real difficulty in reading these materials, one must question whether any more than a minimal level of literacy has been achieved in that school system.

Population II

Passage and Items

Paracutin was born in Mexico in February, 1943. At the end of one week, Paracutin was 500 feet high and it is now over 9 000 feet high. Today Paracutin is asleep.

What is Paracutin? It is the only volcano in the world which has been seen from its birth right up to the present day. On February 20, 1943, a peasant and his wife set out to work in their maize fields from the Mexican village of Paracutin. They were surprised to find the earth warm under their feet. Suddenly they heard noises deep in the earth and a small hollow appeared in their field. In the afternoon there was a sudden loud noise and stones were flung high in the air. The peasants ran from the field and turned to watch. They saw the birth of a volcano.

There were great bursts of stone and lava and a little hill began to form. By evening this hill was 100 feet high and hot ashes were falling on the village. At night the glare of the hot lava lit up the countryside. The trees near the village were killed and the villagers had to leave their houses. When the village was abandoned, its name was given to the volcano. The news quickly spread to Mexico City, far to the east. Many sightseers and scientists flocked to the scene. The volcano grew and grew for ten years and hundreds of square miles of forest were destroyed. Then Paracutin went to sleep. In spite of all the explosions, not one person was killed.

8. Paracutin was once the name of
   A. a peasant.
   B. a village.
   C. an old mountain.
   D. a Mexican.

9. What was destroyed in the eruption?
   A. Only a village
   B. The villagers living close by
   C. The forests and fields around Paracutin
   D. Two peasants

10. When the writer says that Paracutin "went to sleep", he means that it
    A. flattened out.
    B. stopped sending out ashes and lava.
    C. will never be a volcano again.
    D. got covered with grass and trees.

11. In this passage the author is trying to
    A. describe an interesting happening.
    B. explain a scientific story.
    C. make us believe something.
    D. build up suspense.

12. Paracutin is now
    A. erupting.
    B. temporarily inactive.
    C. permanently dead.
    D. flattened.

13. From the story, where does it appear that Paracutin is located?
    A. In eastern Mexico
    B. In western Mexico
    C. In northern Mexico
    D. In southern Mexico

14. What can we learn about volcanoes from this passage?
    A. New volcanoes may appear in unexpected places
    B. There have always been volcanoes on the earth
    C. Volcanoes are active from time to time
    D. Volcanoes are active for only a few months

This straightforward descriptive passage is somewhat easier for 14-year-olds than the passage that was used to illustrate difficulty for Population I was for 10-year-olds. The median of countries and items was an error rate of approximately 30% (Table 8.8). Thus, possibly two thirds of 14-year-olds can read this passage with good understanding of what the author is saying. But this is not true in the three countries (Chile, India and Iran) that have showed up as consistently low in Reading Comprehension score. For them, the median failure rate is, respectively, 47%, 63% and 61%. Remembering that random marking would give 75% of error, one must con-

Table 8.8. *Percent Failing. Population II*

Country	Item 8	Item 9	Item 10	Item 11	Item 12	Item 13	Item 14
Belgium (Fl)	29	14	9	75	37	45	17
Belgium (Fr)	17	8	6	18	42	49	14
Chile	47	25	33	54	57	75	46
England	32	13	15	38	40	40	24
Finland	35	11	10	35	60	46	30
Hungary	30	11	20	46	69	59	26
India	70	36	45	63	73	82	62
Iran	72	24	61	60	54	80	65
Israel	40	30	20	45	48	44	31
Italy	13	10	5	26	42	43	17
Netherlands	33	15	13	30	46	54	20
New Zealand	25	6	13	19	47	36	13
Scotland	30	10	16	23	49	32	21
Sweden	24	13	19	24	68	46	15
United States	21	12	12	33	39	41	20

clude that only a rather small minority of 14-year-olds in these countries are able to read this passage, and the accompanying questions, with anything approaching full comprehension.

Population IV

Passage and Items

During the present century, scientific study of man's surroundings and experiences is commonly accepted as the desirable way to determine the truth or falsity of statements, opinions, or beliefs.

This was not always so. During past centuries there was much reliance on authority. The opinions expressed by persons in positions of authority and the written statements in approved documents were frequently accepted and taught as oracles of truth. Those questioning the accuracy or validity of these opinions were in grave danger. Many persons, later recognized as leading contributors to the progress of mankind, suffered torture, imprisonment, and even death because they dared to question beliefs or opinions which we now see to have been demonstrably false.

The scientific method emphasized the inductive rather than the deductive approach to the solution of problems. The inductive method is characterized by observations, measurement, definitions, enumerations, classification, and the formulation of conclusions on the basis of objective evidence. On the other hand, authoritarianism utilized the deductive method, namely, reasoning from the major premise to a conclusion, without necessarily making explicit all the elements involved in the final statement or opinion.

In one sense authority and scientific method may be harmonized. It is conceivable that the major premises of an authority may be based on scientific studies which have produced demonstrable truths. Deductions made with these truths as major premises and with strict adherence to the principles of logic should be valid.

1. Scientific method has been encouraged
   A. for many centuries.
   B. continuously.
   C. recently.
   D. by authoritarians.

2. "Authority" as used in line 3 of the above article, means
   A. traditional wisdom.
   B. scientific analysis.
   C. inductively determined fact.
   D. superstition.

3. Deductive reasoning assumes the accuracy of
   A. conclusions.
   B. major premises.
   C. facts.
   D. a logical synthesis.

4. A central idea of the preceding article is that
   A. deductive methods are hard to apply.
   B. science and logic are opposed.
   C. facts and opinions are about the same thing.
   D. scientific and authoritarian methods may complement each other.

5. Which of the four paragraphs is primarily concerned with comparison?
   A. 1st
   B. 2nd
   C. 3rd
   D. 4th

6. Which of the four paragraphs is primarily concerned with synthesis?
   A. 1st
   B. 2nd
   C. 3rd
   D. 4th

Table 8.9. *Percent Failing. Population IV*

	Item 1	Item 2	Item 3	Item 4	Item 5	Item 6
Belgium (Fl)	38	21	48	21	28	47
Belgium (Fr)	22	26	41	12	24	18
Chile	48	40	51	25	32	48
England	13	14	40	20	8	48
Finland	16	26	62	15	10	14
Hungary	36	31	49	21	17	46
India	66	65	78	60	65	69
Iran	64	70	78	59	67	74
Israel	23	57	23	20	14	40
Italy	17	22	47	18	28	25
Netherlands	10	25	6	26	9	9
New Zealand	6	10	34	13	10	43
Scotland	14	17	47	23	6	48
Sweden	32	26	54	27	24	53
United States	34	31	54	29	22	59

Finally, data are given for the initial passage in the reading test for students in the final year of secondary education (Table 8.9). This is clearly a relatively abstract passage, compared with those at the earlier levels, and consequently more difficult. However, it would hardly seem to be more difficult than material that secondary school graduates are expected to read. And in most countries the majority of terminal year secondary school students are able to handle it. The median error rate is typically about 25%. This is in most countries a fairly taxing but manageable reading task. Once again, however, one may turn to the three developing countries. Here there are median error rates of 44%, 66% and 68% (for Chile, India and Iran respectively), and the reading task presented by this passage seems to have overwhelmed most students.

VARIABILITY OF PERFORMANCE WITHIN A COUNTRY

Countries may differ not only in average performance, but also in variability of performance. The fact of differences between countries in variability tells one nothing about the causes of these differences. Conceivably, great variability in the reading comprehension of students in a particular country might arise from great heterogeneity in the genetic potential of the population of that country. On the other hand, the great variability may represent a wide variation in educational opportunity and cultural background. Perhaps the typical situation will be that the differences in variability are to some degree a function both of the basic characteristics of the population and of the type and range of both home and school learning opportunities. Some cues as to the extent to which the variability in performance arises from educational causes, as opposed to genetic or cultural variances associated with the family, may be obtained from examining the proportion of the variance that arises between schools (potentially reflecting educational differences) as compared to the proportion that is within a single school (almost certainly reflecting individual biological and cultural differences). The basic data for examining national differences in variability are to be found in Tables 8.1, 8.2 and 8.3 (see pp. 124–126). These tables include the standard deviations for Reading Comprehension, Reading speed, and Word knowledge score for each of the countries.

On the Reading Comprehension test in Populations I and II, all of the English-speaking countries show large standard deviations. Though it is possible that this reflects a genuinely greater diversity within these countries than in others, there is also the possibility that this represents the fact that the basic development of the tests was largely in English, and that the tests were consequently somewhat better and somewhat more discriminating tests in that language. If this were so, it would tend to make sharper discriminations between the more and less able individuals and therefore to spread the scores out over a wider range.

In addition to the English-speaking countries, Israel shows a very sizable standard deviation. This may reasonably be understood in terms of the great diversity of origins of the population of Israel today, with some groups coming from European countries with a strong educational tradition and others from Near Eastern countries in which educational programs have been much more limited. The variability in Iran in Populations I and II and of India in Population II is strikingly smaller than for all of the other countries. This reduced variability is a corollary of the very low means in these countries indicating that the whole distribution of scores is compressed down near to the chance level. The test is functioning in a very different way for the students in these groups than it is in the other countries, producing a substantial piling up of chance and near chance scores.

In Population IV, the country that is dramatically more variable in performance than any of the others is the United States. This is readily understood in the light of the high retention rate in schools in the United States, where roughly three fourths of the age group are still in school at the end of the secondary school program. At the other end, the variability in Iran and India continues to be definitely the least, once again being consistent with the very low mean score in those countries. The country with a relatively high mean score that shows the smallest standard deviation is the Netherlands. Apparently the school population surviving at the end of secondary education is a decidedly homogeneous one in this national group.

Variability patterns in the test of reading speed are quite different from those on the test of comprehension. In the case of reading speed, two of the countries that scored relatively poorly on the comprehension test show very large standard deviations on the speed test. However, these large standard deviations are accompanied by high mean and large standard deviation in number of errors on the speed test. One gets the impression that in Iran and Chile some individuals went through the tests very rapidly with a minimal level of understanding, marking but not really reading and comprehending. This tendency to dash ahead and mark whether one understands or not seems to be even more uniformly the case in India, where the mean speed score is very high but the standard deviation is fairly small. Here again, the high speed is accompanied by a large proportion of error so that one has a feeling that something in the cultural pressure of the testing situation led these youngsters to push ahead and mark a great many items whether they understood what they had been reading or not. The other country that shows high variability on the speed test is Israel, and this is consistent with the results on reading comprehension. Presumably the same explanation applies to both.

The shortcomings of the Word knowledge test in translation make any attempt to interpret the variability on this test somewhat unprofitable. Differences in variability may well merely reflect differences in the effectiveness with which the items were translated into word pairs of appropriate difficulty and differentiating power in the different languages rather than any characteristic of the country per se.

Another aspect of variability is an analysis of the extent to which variation occurs between schools, as opposed to within schools in a country. The greater the proportion of between-school variability, the more heterogeneous the different units of the educational system are, and, conversely, the less variability there is between schools, the more nearly individual talents are spread out evenly over the units of a school system. In order to get an index of this, the between-school variance was expressed as a percentage of the total variance for each country. This was done separately for the Reading Comprehension, Reading speed, and Word knowledge tests. The results are presented in Table 8.10.

The first columns of Table 8.10 show the proportion of variation that was between-school for Reading Comprehension score in Populations I, II and IV as far as the information was available from each of these populations. Between-school variation in Reading Comprehension score is relatively greatest at Population II, and this corresponds to the finding discussed in Chapter 7 that at this level school type is an important predictor of Reading Comprehension score for most countries. Schools tend to be most uniform at the end of the secondary program. In spite of the probable reduction of

Table 8.10. *Proportions of Variance Arising from Differences Among School Means*

Country	Reading Comprehension Population			Reading Speed Population		Word Knowledge Population		
	I	II	IV	I	II	I	II	IV
Belgium (Fl)	31	—	39	48	—	21	—	26
Belgium (Fr)	26	—	33	65	—	31	—	21
Chile	62	51	28	71	53	44	41	27
England	20	33	21	27	31	20	30	18
Finland	23	39	17	46	35	20	29	7
Hungary	31	30	21	42	29	19	16	14
India	82	62	27	82	63	62	67	26
Iran	29	—	22	37	—	16	—	8
Israel	36	54	55	56	50	22	36	35
Italy	53	48	60	42	44	40	47	34
Netherlands	28	43	17	52	36	16	40	15
New Zealand	—	14	9	—	21	—	14	12
Scotland	21	36	17	24	31	24	34	16
Sweden	15	9	36	26	13	14	7	24
United States	26	31	23	25	26	27	28	19
Median	28	38	22	44	33	22	32	18

individual variation at this level, variation between schools has apparently been reduced even more.

The proportion of between-school variance varies rather widely from country to country. In certain countries and at certain levels less than 10% of the total variation occurs between schools, while in one or two instances it goes as high as 60% and in one case even to 80%. In Populations I and II, the country that shows very high variation between schools is India, where as much as 80% of the variation is variation from one school to another in school mean score. Apparently either the input or the educational program is so radically different from school to school in India that the performers within a given school tend to be relatively consistent in their level of achievement, while the differences between schools are very dramatic and striking. By contrast, Sweden tends to show the smallest variation from school to school, with only 10 or 15% of the variation being variation between school means and the other 85 or 90% being variation within schools. Overall, Sweden is not noticeably less variable than other countries. That is, individuals are about as variable in their performance in Sweden as they are in other countries. However, the schools that were tested in the Swedish sample tend to be decidedly uniform in score level and talent tends to be spread with an even hand over the different schools of the country. Another country in which the variability is decidedly low is New Zealand. New Zealand tested only in Populations II and IV, but in both of those populations the variability from school to school is under 15% of the total.

National variations in between-school variability are not easy for the outsider to interpret. They are a joint function of the geographical stratification of the population, the diversity of school types, and the tendency to retain a wide range of talent in the schools. This and possibly other factors interact to make one country have schools that are relatively uniform and other countries schools that are highly diverse.

The last section of Table 8.10 shows the proportion of variance that is between-school variance on the Word knowledge test. Results in this case tend to be consistent with those for the Reading Comprehension test. That is, countries that show low between-school variability in the one case tend to show it also in the other. Low variability appears in Sweden and in New Zealand and high variability appears in India, while the other countries tend in general to be intermediate. It is generally but not universally true that the between-school variance is a smaller proportion of the total for the Word knowledge test than it is for the Reading Comprehension test. This seems reasonable if the Word knowledge test is more nearly a measure of the basic ability of the individual in question, and the Reading Comprehension test more a function of the skills that he was specifically taught in school. One would expect that school groups would vary more greatly in school-taught skills than in basic ability levels, since variation in effectiveness of the school's program of instruction would be added to the original variation in input. The results available here seem to be consistent with this interpretation.

Proportion-of-variance data for Reading speed scores tend roughly to parallel those for Reading Comprehension. However, it is interesting that between-school variance tended to be greater for speed in Population I and for comprehension in Population II. One can only speculate as to the reasons, but it seems likely that the emphasis in directions given to students and the accuracy of timing a four-minute test might constitute significant sources of between-school variance on the speed test, while between-school variance on the comprehension test is more a function of selectivity in the input to different schools.

INCREMENTS IN ACHIEVEMENT FROM POPULATION I TO POPULATIONS II AND IV

In order to make it possible to study increments in achievement from age 10 to age 14 and on to the end of secondary education, some common "anchor" items were included in the tests of adjoining levels. The increment in achievement was estimated by the following procedure:

1. Population II was used as the "anchor" population, and increments were expressed in every case in terms of the mean and standard deviation of Population II.

2. The average standard deviation of true scores on the anchor items was estimated using the formula

$$\hat{\bar{\sigma}}_{x_\infty} = \bar{S}_x \sqrt{\bar{r}_{xx'}}$$

3. For each country, the quantities

$$\frac{(\bar{X}_2 - \bar{X}_1)\,100}{\hat{\bar{\sigma}}_{x_\infty}} \text{ and } \frac{(\bar{X}_4 - \bar{X}_2)\,100}{\hat{\bar{\sigma}}_{x_\infty}}$$

were calculated.

Recognizing the limitations of conclusions based on such a fragile bridge from one level to the next, one may say from the data available (see Table 8.11) that there is an average gain in reading from age 10 to age 14 of about one and a quarter standard deviations of the 14-year-old group, and a gain from 14 to the end of secondary school of about one and a half standard deviations. This could be expressed differently by saying that the average 10-year-old would fall at about the 10th percentile of 14-year-olds (and, conversely that about 10% of the 14-year-olds would do no better than the average 10-year-old), while the average student in the final year of secondary education would fall at about the 93rd percentile of 14-year-olds.

There are rather wide differences from country to country in indicated amount of gain. The gains in India and Iran fall far below those in all other countries. Progress in reading ability seems to be very slow in these two countries. They start below the other countries and fall further and further behind. In amount of progress, Italy also falls well below the remaining countries, but in this case the starting point is one of the highest of any of the countries tested. This is in

Table 8.11. *Increments in Achievement from Population I to Population II to Population IV, Expressed in Standard Score Units of Population II*

Country	Reading Comprehension Population			Word Knowledge Population		
	I to II	II to IV	I to IV	I to II	II to IV	I to IV
Belgium (Fl)	1.36	1.11	2.47	1.14	0.34	1.48
Belgium (Fr)	1.34	1.48	2.82	1.34	1.78	3.12
Chile	0.79	1.61	2.40	0.53	1.57	2.10
England	1.09	2.04	3.13	1.20	2.28	3.48
Finland	1.23	1.46	2.69	—[b]	—[b]	—[b]
Hungary	1.51	1.17	2.68	1.06	0.88	1.94
India	0.15	0.39	0.54	−.08	0.60	0.52
Iran	0.60	0.22	0.82	1.39	1.34	2.73
Israel	1.38	1.36	2.74	1.12	0.28	1.40
Italy	0.61	1.02	1.63	0.79	1.52	2.31
Netherlands	1.23	2.11	3.34	1.03	1.89	2.92
New Zealand	—[a]	1.76	—[a]	—[a]	2.22	—[a]
Scotland	1.49	1.84	3.33	1.50	2.19	3.69
Sweden	1.26	1.60	2.86	0.95	1.69	2.64
United States	1.78	0.87	2.65	1.38	0.75	2.13
Median	1.24	1.46	2.68	1.12	1.54	2.31

[a] New Zealand did not test Population I.
[b] The Word knowledge test in Finland was locally produced and does not conform to the test used in the other countries.

part because a fifth grade group was used and about 20 % of the 10-year-olds that were in the fourth or lower grades were excluded. In the remaining countries, size of gain matches rather closely the degree of selectivity of the school system. Thus, the United States shows the smallest increment from the age of 14 to the end of secondary school of the remaining countries, reflecting the fact that retention of students in school through this period is reported to be higher in the United States than in any of the other reporting countries.

Gains in Word knowledge scores appear to be comparable to, though perhaps slightly less than gains in Reading Comprehension scores. In general, the countries that show larger gains in the one measure also show larger gains in the other, the rank-difference correlation being 0.69.

The one substantial discrepancy occurred for Iran, which showed a gain of only 0.82 standard deviation units for Reading Compre-

145

hension but a gain of 2.73 standard deviation units for Word knowledge. It appears that Iranian students make good progress in acquiring mastery of the single words of their language, but relatively little in the skills of reading connected prose. It is not easy to say why this is so.

PREDICTORS OF NATIONAL DIFFERENCES IN AVERAGE READING SCORE

One would like to know what it is about a country and its educational system that produces, or at least is associated with high reading achievement on the part of students in that country. Unfortunately, countries and their educational systems differ in a great many respects, and information was gathered in this study on a total of only 15 countries. Thus, within the multitude of associations between national characteristics and reading achievement, it is clearly not possible to identify those differences that are fundamental and those differences that are incidental. The most dramatic differences in achievement are those between the 12 relatively economically developed countries and the three at a less advanced stage of development, and hence any national variables that are signs of economic development are likely to be related to achievement in the total group of 15 countries. The question that remains is whether there are factors associated with national differences in achievement within the group of 12 economically developed countries.

An exhaustive analysis has not yet been made of this issue, in part because of the large number of possible variables and the small number of countries. Some of the variables that were found to be predictive of differences in achievement of single students *within* countries were taken and national differences in average level on these variables were correlated with average Reading Comprehension scores. This analysis has been carried out for the 14-year-olds of Population II, and the results are presented in Table 8.12. Correlations are presented for all 15 countries, and also for only the 12 developed countries.

As might have been anticipated, when all 15 countries are included a number of the correlations are quite large. This is the case not only for Father's education and Mother's education (0.60 and 0.73), but also for Number of books in the home (0.85) and Hours listening to radio or watching television (0.92). Indices that relate to information resources, both written and oral, seem to be

Table 8.12. *Correlations of Country Mean Reading Comprehension with Other National Variables. Population II*

Variable	All 15 Countries	12 Developed Countries
Father's education	.60	.14
Mother's education	.73	.23
Expected education	.67	.30
Hours homework weekly	.25	.19
Hours instruction—mother tongue	.21	.47
Parents help with homework	.53	.13
Parents encourage to read	.56	.04
Parents interested in school	.07	.12
Dictionary available	.09	.25
Number of books in home	.85	.17
Number of magazines	.71	.36
Hours radio or TV	.92	.28
Frequency movie attendance	.23	.07
Hours reading for pleasure	.16	.29

the most highly related to achievement in this diverse set of countries.

When correlations are based solely on the economically developed countries, the picture is rather different. Correlations are all quite modest, the largest being a correlation of 0.47 with Hours of instruction in the mother tongue. Second is Number of magazines in the home (0.36), followed by Expected years of education (0.30). Most of the variables that are positively correlated with individual achievement within a country do show positive correlations across countries. Thus, reading achievement tends to be higher in countries where there is more education for fathers (0.14), more education for mothers (0.23), more frequent availability of a dictionary (0.25), more books (0.17), more magazines (0.36), and more parental interest (0.12). Also, all the indicators of involvement in education and communication on the part of students, such as Expected further education (0.30), Reading for pleasure (0.29), Radio and TV listening (0.28) and Movie attendance (0.07), show modest positive correlations.

Many other items of information about the country or its schools might have been analyzed in relation to reading achievement. Because of the limited group of countries, the present analysis has been limited to these few variables and to the 14-year-old group.

SUMMARY

The most dramatic feature of the between-country results is the very large difference between the developed countries with a strong system of universal education and the developing countries. The differences are of a size such that only 5 or 10% of students in a developing country score as well on a test of reading comprehension as the average student in one of the developed countries. Of course, part of the difference may stem from unfamiliarity with objective test formats. But the report of representatives of the developing countries indicate that this is probably a minor matter, and that the tasks were genuinely too difficult for students in those countries. The reasons may be found in part in the schools, where meager material resources and teachers with a minimal training and background lead to a limited educational program, but they probably lie more in the home and the society, where resources for verbal and intellectual stimulation are meager at best.

Retentivity becomes an important factor in a country's performance in the group at the end of secondary education. Because of difficulties in estimating how much of an impact differences in retentivity have had, cross-national comparisons become difficult to interpret in Population IV.

The differences among developed countries are of rather modest dimensions. Though a given country may be gratified or concerned that it does a little better or worse than the overall averages, the variations do not seem very important or readily interpretable.

Chapter 9

Consistency of Test Characteristics from Country to Country

In this chapter an examination will be made of the evidence from the study that bears upon the extent to which the tests displayed the same characteristics in the different countries. The evidence gathered on this consists primarily of the correlations of item difficulty and item discrimination indices from one country to another. To the extent that the same items are hard and the same items are discriminating in different countries and different languages, one can have some feeling of assurance that the test is functioning in the same way in each and that it can be thought of as roughly an equivalent test. This type of evidence is not definitive, but it is at least suggestive.

Another type of evidence that is worth examination is the types of misleads or distractors that were attractive to individuals in different countries. The question asked here is whether there are substantial numbers of instances in which an item choice that tended to be chosen frequently in most countries was not chosen in a particular country, or whether there are cases in which a mislead that was rarely chosen in most countries showed a very heavy preponderance of choices in one particular country. Where instances of this sort arise, one must ask why they appeared. In general, two kinds of possibilities suggest themselves as explanations of such variation. On the one hand, there are the problems of translation. It may be that the passage as a whole or some of the words in it carried a somewhat different connotation in one language from what it did in the others, or it may be that the questions or the wording of the choices to an item had a somewhat different flavor from one language to another. The other possibility would seem to be that the culture and expectations of the country differed from that of others so that a response that seemed somehow plausible in one culture seemed inappropriate and unsuitable in another.

With respect to the first type of evidence mentioned above, one can consider the correlations among the items across countries. In this case the 45, 52 or 54 items serve as the members of a population of items, and the difficulty or discrimination indices represent the "score" that the item obtained in each country. These scores were correlated across countries as if they were scores on a number of different tests by a group of persons. In this instance, the country corresponds to the test and the item corresponds to the person. Once the correlations are available, one can look at them either by inspection, or somewhat more systematically by the techniques of factor analysis, and analyses of both types have been carried out. These results are discussed in the first part of what follows.

When it comes to examining the difficulty levels of single items and of the distractors to them in each country, one must first of all adjust the results for the general level of reading performance in each of the different countries. Certain of the countries found the test notably more difficult than the remaining countries, and consequently they would be expected to be high on error responses on a very large number of the items. A multiplier was determined for each country based upon the average difficulty of the items for that country, and the error percentages were adjusted for each country by using the corresponding multiplier. The average proportion (averaged across countries) choosing any given answer to any given item was then found, and the proportion in each country compared with that average value. Whenever the discrepancy was more than a specified amount (the arbitrary figure of 10% was used as a very noticeable difference and 5% as a lower standard of difference) the response was noted as one calling for attention and explanation. For each country a list was prepared of the response options on which that country deviated noticeably from the average of all countries, and the list was sent to the National Center of the country with a request for an interpretation of as many of the differences as they seemed to find a plausible rationale for. The responses to this request have been examined and an attempt has been made to classify the reasons that were given as a basis for difference between the percent in a particular country and the overall average percentage. These are discussed in the final sections of the chapter.

DIFFICULTY AND DISCRIMINATION ANALYSIS

The correlations of Reading Comprehension difficulty indices and discrimination indices across countries are shown in Tables 9.1, 9.2,

Table 9.1. *Correlations of Item Difficulty Indices and Discrimination Indices. Population I*

(Difficulty Indices above Diagonal and Discrimination Indices below Diagonal)

Country	Belgium (Fl)	Belgium (Fr)	Chile	England	Finland	Hungary	India	Iran	Israel	Italy	Netherlands	Scotland	Sweden	United States	Mean Difficulty	SD Difficulty
Belgium (Fl)	—	80	74	84	80	74	74	51	73	80	90	84	83	68	54	20
Belgium (Fr)	57	—	76	77	80	78	71	52	81	86	80	79	77	72	54	20
Chile	45	66	—	78	72	78	78	55	74	62	76	77	77	74	39	14
England	65	71	77	—	86	79	79	62	72	74	88	98	83	91	56	15
Finland	59	68	69	74	—	82	77	55	78	72	80	85	79	78	57	18
Hungary	61	52	64	68	69	—	72	58	73	68	79	78	70	73	48	19
India	26	61	67	62	52	58	—	60	81	73	70	80	79	75	38	15
Iran	21	43	63	56	39	61	73	—	63	49	56	67	60	57	29	11
Israel	65	76	67	72	75	74	70	47	—	76	75	75	75	66	47	17
Italy	56	62	41	54	55	60	40	28	63	—	78	74	73	65	60	20
Netherlands	65	53	70	75	63	70	48	57	62	49	—	88	87	78	54	20
Scotland	69	73	78	96	76	69	59	55	78	56	76	—	84	91	55	16
Sweden	46	54	78	73	63	58	42	51	48	41	76	72	—	73	60	18
United States	54	55	76	81	58	69	60	56	65	38	68	79	58	—	53	16
Mean Discrimination	34	35	34	42	40	35	34	27	41	37	35	40	40	41		
SD Discrimination	11	13	15	12	12	14	15	12	15	13	14	13	12	11		

151

Table 9.2. *Correlations of Item Difficulty Indices and Discrimination Indices. Population II*

(Difficulty Indices above Diagonal and Discrimination Indices below Diagonal)

Country	Belgium (Fl)	Belgium (Fr)	Chile	England	Finland	Hungary	India	Iran	Israel	Italy	Netherlands	New Zealand	Scotland	Sweden	United States	Mean Difficulty	SD Difficulty
Belgium (Fl)	—	57	70	85	74	66	49	41	77	74	84	80	82	83	77	60	21
Belgium (Fr)	32	—	51	66	76	52	52	42	54	63	66	65	66	66	65	64	21
Chile	46	08	—	83	67	63	64	55	82	70	72	79	80	73	76	45	16
England	52	44	50	—	78	62	56	47	84	77	83	94	98	85	85	61	18
Finland	52	55	33	57	—	77	55	48	68	69	84	75	79	83	69	64	17
Hungary	38	39	48	46	62	—	53	40	66	58	76	62	62	76	55	62	19
India	15	-11	41	20	20	07	—	77	62	56	46	56	53	57	59	32	14
Iran	35	36	35	26	29	33	44	—	50	43	39	43	42	44	51	35	16
Israel	62	42	57	60	60	52	10	23	—	76	76	80	83	75	72	57	16
Italy	37	45	31	42	62	42	13	13	48	—	70	76	77	68	71	65	20
Netherlands	62	49	33	51	56	46	14	41	54	33	—	82	85	86	75	61	20
New Zealand	43	50	40	85	67	44	14	12	58	58	46	—	95	85	91	67	18
Scotland	50	50	43	94	62	40	12	22	57	44	54	89	—	86	84	64	19
Sweden	56	38	32	70	57	27	18	20	39	36	40	70	70	—	78	62	21
United States	39	42	35	70	56	31	32	37	40	46	47	76	71	68	—	64	18
Mean Discrimination	32	29	34	38	36	32	23	22	40	31	33	37	38	36	38		
SD Discrimination	10	11	11	11	09	09	11	09	11	09	09	09	11	10	11		

Table 9.3. *Correlations of Item Difficulty Indices and Item Discrimination Indices. Population IV*

(Difficulty Indices above Diagonal and Discrimination Indices below Diagonal)

Country	Belgium (Fl)	Belgium (Fr)	Chile	England	Finland	Hungary	India	Iran	Israel	Italy	Netherlands	New Zealand	Scotland	Sweden	United States	Mean Difficulty	SD Difficulty
Belgium (Fl)	—	62	42	67	59	50	26	47	48	57	53	69	69	54	60	59	20
Belgium (Fr)	45	—	74	77	81	68	48	56	71	73	75	76	76	74	82	63	18
Chile	31	69	—	67	60	56	49	54	72	54	53	63	63	63	74	46	18
England	44	79	49	—	79	72	41	53	72	72	65	96	97	70	84	71	17
Finland	54	59	40	68	—	83	50	55	61	68	67	72	79	75	79	66	22
Hungary	41	67	54	61	61	—	52	53	60	60	51	64	73	69	66	58	21
India	-02	02	29	-12	-11	-11	—	48	49	34	35	35	41	42	44	28	10
Iran	-09	18	49	08	08	09	49	—	60	49	54	47	54	55	54	29	13
Israel	10	54	56	40	34	42	25	40	—	66	68	72	69	51	68	59	19
Italy	35	63	56	44	44	58	20	35	60	—	70	73	72	54	76	58	22
Netherlands	39	68	48	61	49	39	08	05	47	46	—	66	65	59	63	68	24
New Zealand	35	73	41	88	67	52	-09	08	38	35	62	—	94	67	83	74	17
Scotland	50	67	31	89	62	52	-19	-13	29	36	55	79	—	75	84	73	18
Sweden	46	66	48	68	66	74	-16	07	35	46	58	67	60	—	81	62	19
United States	39	69	63	66	55	60	05	18	56	55	47	62	53	54	—	55	17
Mean Discrimination	28	29	28	31	26	28	19	21	34	32	26	29	28	30	36		
SD Discrimination	12	10	09	09	08	09	09	11	14	14	09	08	10	10	13		

153

and 9.3 for the three populations of individuals from whom data were obtained. In each table the difficulty indices appear above the diagonal and the discrimination indices appear below the diagonal. Table 9.1 shows the correlational data for ten-year-olds. In this instance, the median correlation of difficulty indices between countries in which a different language was spoken was 0.75. The median correlation for the discrimination indices was 0.62. Much higher correlations were obtained between the three English-speaking countries and the correlations between England and Scotland reached the very high values of 0.98 for difficulty and 0.96 for discrimination. These last correlations might be thought of as representing reliability coefficients based on two samples from a common population, and give some indication of the stability of the difficulty and discrimination indices when they are based upon samples of the size that were tested in those two countries. Thus, one can accept the difficulty and discrimination indices as being rather dependable values for a particular country, and recognize that the lower correlations in countries speaking different languages must be thought of as representing a shifting of difficulty or discrimination of the tasks as one passes from one language to another. The correlations of the order of 0.75 do indicate that there is a substantial consistency in the relative difficulty of the tasks represented by the test items as one goes from country to country, so that the items that are hardest in one country tend also to be hardest in the other. This is true particularly among the developed countries, and one finds in particular that the correlations involving Iran are noticeably lower than those for the remaining countries. This can be understood as due in part to the fact that a substantial number of items on the test were responded to at no better than a chance level by the students in Iran, and to the fact that the spread of item difficulties was less in Iran than in any of the other countries.

The consistency of the discrimination indices from country to country was noticeably lower than that of the difficulty indices. However, this may indicate nothing more profound than the fact that items were chosen with the objective of getting a wide range of levels of difficulty but of maintaining a uniformly high level of discrimination.

How is one to interpret consistency of the sort found for this set of data? One certainly might hope that the consistency would be higher than this, and the earlier pilot study of reading among 13-year-olds carried out in a number of the same countries (Foshay,

Table 9.4. *Rotated Factor Loadings for Reading Comprehension Test. Population I*

Country	Difficulty			Discrimination		
	I	II	III	I	II	III
Belgium (Fl)	93	−02	12	75	21	*35*
Belgium (Fr)	86	10	*35*	77	14	*48*
Chile	79	*33*	11	80	28	11
English[a]	86	28	02	85	16	14
Finland	83	28	23	84	00	*35*
Hungary	78	*36*	17	80	20	*36*
India	76	*40*	15	58	*64*	*37*
Iran	59	*43*	−03	51	*69*	08
Israel	79	29	*31*	84	17	*54*
Italy	84	−08	*42*	67	01	*57*
Netherlands	96	03	−02	82	09	04
Sweden	91	15	05	76	08	−15

[a] Pooled average of England, Scotland and the United States.

op. cit.) suggested that the correlations would be more nearly of the order of 0.90. One must wonder why as much drop occurred from that earlier study to this one. Is it a question of having items more nearly homogeneous in difficulty in the present test? Is it due to the inclusion of a somewhat more diverse set of countries and languages? These points will be examined a little further.

Factor analyses were carried out for the difficulty and for the discrimination data for this group. However, before carrying out the analysis, data from the three English-speaking countries were pooled and the average of the correlations of the three with each of the other countries was entered into the matrix. It was very apparent that there would be an additional factor of common language for the three English-speaking countries, and in order to analyze the structure of the relationships it seemed better to treat the three as just a single country. The results of the factor analysis are shown in Table 9.4 for Population I. The results bring out rather clearly that the vast bulk of what is common to any pair of countries is common to all of them so far as the difficulty of the tasks is concerned. There are only very small factors beyond the first.

Factor II appears primarily in the two Asiatic countries, Iran and India. Factor III has its largest loading in the two Romance-language European countries, Italy and French-speaking Belgium, with some

Table 9.5. *Rotated Factor Loadings for Reading Comprehension Test. Population II*

Country	Difficulty				Discrimination			
	I	II	III	IV	I	II	III	IV
Belgium (Fl)	90	03	−07	−04	72	15	−06	−04
Belgium (Fr)	65	*53*	17	21	48	*32*	*53*	15
Chile	84	−18	24	08	51	*34*	*−48*	−20
English[a]	89	00	07	13	79	09	00	16
Finland	84	*37*	06	05	72	*34*	19	−01
Hungary	77	15	06	*−33*	71	04	−14	*31*
India	59	04	*65*	−03	16	*38*	*−46*	17
Iran	46	06	*74*	−14	28	*55*	−18	*33*
Israel	88	−15	15	08	67	*32*	10	*32*
Italy	81	06	12	25	58	23	23	−23
Netherlands	91	18	−09	−06	63	*32*	13	07
Sweden	90	18	01	−12	79	−11	−07	21

[a] Pooled average of England, New Zealand, Scotland, and the United States.

loading in Israel. The factor pattern for the discrimination indices corresponds in general to that for the difficulty indices, but the loadings for the second and third factors are noticeably larger than in the case of difficulty.

Tables 9.2 and 9.5 present the correlations and factor analyses for Population II. The consistency from country to country is somewhat less, especially for the discrimination indices. The median cross-language correlation is 0.70 for difficulty but only 0.42 for discrimination. However, it continues to be difficult to make sense of factors beyond the first. There does seem to be a tendency for the two Asiatic countries, India and Iran, to be similar to each other and different from the remaining countries. This pairing shows up especially for the difficulty of items. The affiliation may stem from the fact that Hindi and Persian are both Indo-Iranian languages. However, this pairing may merely reflect the fact that the tests were very difficult in these two countries, with many items responded to at a chance level. The factorial organization of the discrimination indices is more complex, and not easy to rationalize. About half of the countries show up with small loadings on a second factor, but it is far from clear what they have in common. Interpretation of the third and fourth factors is likewise obscure.

For Population IV, the correlations of difficulty indices between

Table 9.6. *Rotated Factor Loadings for Reading Comprehension Test. Population IV*

Country	Difficulty				Discrimination		
	I	II	III	IV	I	II	III
Belgium (Fl)	61	*42*	−10	−27	56	−09	29
Belgium (Fr)	84	29	15	08	83	27	07
Chile	76	04	27	−13	55	*57*	23
English[a]	78	*42*	07	−08	81	02	04
Finland	72	*50*	27	15	73	−01	*31*
Hungary	60	*48*	*44*	04	71	12	*31*
India	50	−03	*49*	−01	−15	*64*	07
Iran	68	00	*30*	−06	−02	*73*	16
Israel	86	−04	13	−04	49	*58*	−12
Italy	79	28	−13	07	58	*50*	04
Netherlands	82	16	−09	24	75	16	−12
Sweden	63	*44*	*34*	01	78	−06	*35*

[a] Pooled average of England, New Zealand, Scotland, and the United States.

countries are again smaller, showing an average value across languages of 0.64. The correlations of discrimination indices are somewhat greater than in Population II, averaging 0.46. The factor analytic results for difficulty make a little better sense at this level. Factor II has appreciable loadings only in the Germanic and Finno-Ugric languages. Factor III appears in India and Iran, but also in Hungary, while Factor IV is inconsequential. For discrimination, a sizable second factor appears, having its largest loadings for India and Iran, but also showing substantial loadings for Chile, Israel and Italy. The logic of this grouping is far from clear. Small loadings of the third factor appear in Finland, Hungary and Sweden (see Table 9.6).

Considering the data as a whole, a moderate amount of consistency in item difficulty has been found from one language to another, but still enough variation to occasion some concern about the comparability of the task presented by the test in its translation into 12 languages. The consistency is less at the higher levels. It is perhaps not surprising that translation makes more of a difference for the more difficult ideas and more complex language of the higher level tests. With the most difficult passages it is even possible that translators had difficulty in fully comprehending the ideas of the original passage and rendering them accurately in the new language.

Table 9.7. *Rotated Factor Loadings for Word Knowledge Test. Population I*

Country	Difficulty I	II	III	IV	Discrimination I	II	III	IV
Belgium (Fl)	13	*60*	23	*52*	*33*	*44*	*46*	06
Belgium (Fr)	11	*43*	17	*75*	29	*44*	*63*	−04
Chile	*71*	*31*	*32*	*41*	*47*	*43*	*33*	−21
England	24	*87*	23	23	*93*	06	23	01
FRG	*41*	−05	05	*72*	−04	03	22	−*69*
Finland	14	10	*81*	20	*33*	07	*53*	*39*
Hungary	*72*	28	11	*34*	15	*67*	19	07
India	*72*	17	*45*	*31*	04	*62*	06	14
Iran	*86*	23	19	06	10	*73*	−*46*	20
Israel	26	19	*78*	05	−10	14	*30*	*70*
Italy	*42*	*36*	*55*	*41*	*54*	25	*46*	01
Netherlands	16	*31*	*50*	*58*	08	01	*78*	−05
Scotland	20	*84*	25	19	*88*	20	23	06
Sweden	*35*	35	24	*59*	−01	*65*	20	−*30*
United States	27	*89*	04	10	*90*	−01	−07	−01

Correlation and factor analyses were also carried out for the Word knowledge test described in Chapter 2, and for which reliability and correlational data are presented in Chapter 4. The rotated factor loadings are presented in Tables 9.7, 9.8 and 9.9 for the three populations. In these analyses, the English-speaking countries have all been entered as variables, with the result that an "English-language factor" appears in each analysis.

In contrast to the results for the Reading Comprehension test, there is little evidence of a single general factor tying together the difficulty and discrimination indices for all countries. Though loadings on any one factor are predominantly of the same sign, implying generally positive correlations across countries, rather pronounced clustering of countries into small groups is typical. However, apart from the fact that the English-speaking countries uniformly appear with loadings on some one factor, it is hard to see any clear rationale for the grouping of countries on a single factor. Occasionally a "sensible" cluster appears, as for example a Romance-languages cluster in Factor II of difficulty for Population IV, but such clusters with a simple rationale are the exception.

Difficulties in equating the Word knowledge test in different countries were noted in Chapter 2. The lack of a clear common

Table 9.8. *Rotated Factor Loadings for Word Knowledge Test. Population II*

Country	Difficulty				Discrimination			
	I	II	III	IV	I	II	III	IV
Australia	*93*	27	13	03	*95*	05	15	05
Belgium (Fl)	16	*78*	12	− 30	*36*	05	*54*	16
Belgium (Fr)	*66*	*33*	*32*	− 11	− 04	*69*	01	07
Chile	*38*	*50*	*53*	− 08	24	− 42	15	*70*
England	*91*	26	20	03	*95*	− 06	00	12
FRG	25	*65*	− 08	*39*	− 11	18	*44*	*53*
Finland	04	08	10	*93*	− 29	06	*45*	08
Hungary	*32*	*66*	− 06	− 05	*37*	− 24	*61*	− 09
India	− 08	*80*	05	18	29	05	*54*	− 30
Iran	24	*57*	15	00	15	09	− 12	*70*
Israel	16	04	*74*	07	04	− 78	00	14
Italy	14	03	*79*	03	− 11	− 70	− 11	− 08
Netherlands	*31*	*59*	01	22	10	19	*72*	00
New Zealand	*96*	21	12	04	*91*	01	12	06
Scotland	*94*	15	18	08	*95*	02	10	− 07
Sweden	*34*	*61*	22	00	05	− 37	*52*	20
United States	*94*	22	10	05	*87*	− 05	16	23

Table 9.9. *Rotated Factor Loadings for Word Knowledge Test. Population IV*

Country	Difficulty				Discrimination			
	I	II	III	IV	I	II	III	IV
Australia	*94*	14	15	11	*93*	08	00	11
Belgium (Fl)	*32*	04	18	*74*	14	*41*	− 11	− 04
Belgium (Fr)	*45*	*50*	15	− 31	29	21	*77*	28
Chile	24	*52*	− 02	18	18	18	13	*75*
England	*91*	09	05	*30*	*84*	*34*	05	17
FRG	03	07	*33*	17	− 16	28	− 62	26
Finland	27	− 19	*64*	− 28	− 18	10	18	− 11
France	16	*86*	04	− 24	*53*	29	*45*	21
Hungary	09	− 11	*63*	02	− 19	*73*	19	− 13
India	− 11	24	*68*	*30*	− 20	− 23	*51*	06
Iran	*38*	*34*	06	*34*	08	− 20	− 03	*71*
Israel	*43*	07	− 35	− 04	06	*54*	14	26
Italy	− 02	*80*	− 06	13	05	*41*	*60*	11
Netherlands	20	− 06	10	*87*	19	*83*	− 09	− 04
New Zealand	*92*	13	06	24	*91*	04	03	22
Scotland	*93*	10	06	26	*85*	00	24	16
Sweden	*33*	11	*34*	*32*	*49*	*39*	*34*	− 29
United States	*84*	16	16	03	*58*	− 03	− 12	− 14

factor or reasonable group of factors in the analysis of item difficulty and discrimination confirms the doubts expressed about the comparability of this test from country to country.

JUDGMENTS OF ITEM RESPONSES

Attention is now turned to an attempt to understand the reasons for discrepancies between countries in their responses to the test items. This has been done primarily through an examination of the frequency with which the three wrong responses were chosen, in the belief that if it were possible to understand why certain error choices were particulary attractive in a certain country one could at the same time understand why the item as a whole was especially easy or difficult for that country. The error responses were examined in two ways. In the first of these, items were identified that had either an especially large number of sizable variations from country to country or an especially small number. The items were then examined to see whether the two groups tended to differ in well defined ways. In the second approach, a national representative was asked to examine those instances in which the popularity of an error choice for his country differed markedly from the popularity of that same error choice for all countries. (An adjustment was first made for average level of Reading Comprehension test score in each country.) He was asked to suggest a hypothesis as to the reason for each difference. These reasons were examined, and were coded as well as possible into categories relating to (1) translation difficulties or errors, (2) specific characteristics of the language, or (3) specific features of the culture. Many instances did not lend themselves to coding because (1) no hypothesis was suggested, (2) the hypothesis seemed to apply to all countries rather than to the specific country, or (3) the hypothesis did not seem to fit any of the categories.

When the items that showed the greatest variation from country to country were compared with those that showed the least, one characteristic on which the two groups of items differed sharply was their level of difficulty. The variable items were quite generally difficult items, while the uniform items were usually easy items. However, this may be a rather superficial relationship, since proportions choosing one specific wrong response could only vary substantially if there were a good many errors being made. That is, the fewer the errors on average, the less opportunity there is for variations in error rates to appear.

An examination of the items themselves provided some suggestions as to content elements that may have been associated with variability, but no systematic checking of these cues was carried out to verify that the indicators were in fact more characteristic of variable items than of stable ones. They are offered in the following paragraphs as very tentative suggestions.

1. A number of the variable items appeared to depend very heavily upon one or two key words. It seems likely that these may have been difficult to translate precisely and/or at the same level of difficulty. Thus, in one item dogs are spoken of as being "savage." Another requires knowledge that the term "mammalia" refers to horses, bears or tigers, but not to dinosaurs. A third asks for the meaning of "authority" as used in a specific context. An unabridged dictionary gives eight distinguishable definitions for "authority" in English. It seems likely that the translated equivalent for the particular meaning used in this passage may have a good many fewer alternate meanings than exist for the English word, and that the alternatives may not match the error choices as closely as was true in English. Still another requires knowledge that when camels are "stampeded" they are driven off, and not killed, seized or ridden away. The experience of developing the Word knowledge test had indicated the difficulty of producing word knowledge items of equivalent difficulty in various languages, so that it came as no surprise that a number of the more variable reading items appeared to depend heavily upon knowledge of the meaning of a specific word.

2. Several of the most variable items called for interpretation of the feelings or motivation of either a character in the passage or the author. Thus an item asks whether a girl felt amused, angry or embarrassed. (The correct response was "We cannot tell.") Ten-year-olds in different countries differed widely in their tendency to attribute amusement vs. embarrassment to the girl. Another item asks about the "writer's feelings about the musk ox." Still another asks about the author's purpose, i.e. "the writer of this passage is trying to present ..." Thus, there is a suggestion that cultural differences in interpretation of motivations and emotions may be an occasional source of variation in response.

3. Finally, a number of the more variable items appear to be ones that require inference beyond what is directly given in the passage,

while the more stable items deal with the directly given. This feature is probably confounded with the aspect of difficulty, since inference items tend to be harder and specific fact items to be easier. However, the tendency to find more variability in inference items seems a reasonable finding. Inference items by their very nature depend more upon what the individual himself brings to the task, and are less completely structured by the passage itself. Hence, one would expect differences in national culture to play a larger role for the inference items.

The second approach to trying to account for the variability of response to items in different countries was to have the National Technical Officer or National Reading Committee review those choices that were made disproportionately often or seldom in the country in question and "psychologize" on the item, offering an explanation of the deviant response. It was suggested to those who reviewed the choices that likely categories for explanation were (1) some inherent characteristic of the language itself, such as its specific vocabulary or some aspect of its syntactic structure, (2) a problem arising out of the particular translation that was made of the original English version, a characteristic that was peculiar to the translator rather than inherent in the language, and (3) differences that represented aspects of the national culture, such as emphasis on certain values or different patterns of educational experience. In addition to the above three categories, reviewers were invited to indicate some other rationale for the peculiar response in their country or to agree that they had no good rationale for the way the item had behaved.

Materials were received back from some but not all of the countries, and this is understandable because making the judgments asked for was a time-consuming and frustrating enterprise. The author, who tried to rationalize the idiosyncrasies of response in the United States, can testify to the difficulty of the task. Those responses that were received were examined in relation to the types of categories proposed above and for any further insights that they seemed to provide. The results of this analysis are set forth in the following paragraphs.

The first thing that became clear was that there were large numbers of deviations for which the national representatives found it difficult or impossible to generate a satisfying rationale. In some instances, reasons were given why an option was difficult, but not a reason as to why it was more difficult in the particular country responding than it would have been in other countries. These reactions, though interesting, were not helpful for the specific purpose of explaining differences between countries, and had to be classified as "no explanation." Of course, some of the differences may have arisen on a relatively random basis since differences of 5 % or so in proportion choosing a particular wrong answer might occur from time to time by chance in a fairly long set of items. But it is also true that in many instances any attempt to account for an observed difference was fairly farfetched.

A fair number of instances were reported where the difference seemed to be a matter of the translation or reproduction of the item. Unfortunately, there were one or two instances of gross error, in which the order of response choices was switched or the numbering of responses was omitted, and these produced gross distortions in performance on that item that were not discovered until the final stage of checking the item statistics at the conclusion of the enterprise. As far as one can tell, such events did not happen in more than one item in any given country, but they do represent a penalty of almost a full point for students in a country in which the options were switched around and the presumably right response was in fact a wrong response on the booklet that the students received.

Much more frequent were instances where the national reviewer felt that a better choice of words would have been possible or that the word used conveyed a somewhat different impression from the English original. This is perhaps to be expected, and is consistent with the earlier report that some of the items with the largest discrepancies were items that depended critically upon a single word or phrase.

Finally, there were a number of items in which the reviewers suggested that a cultural factor was at work. This happened fairly frequently in a country like India, where the climate, the general pattern of life, and to some extent the philosophy of the local culture were inconsistent with the basically European pattern that generated most of the passages and items. Again, a country like Finland found passages dealing with life in the far north somewhat more locally relevant and familiar than was true of other countries. Thus, it did appear that an appreciable number of discrepancies reflected something of the general background of the students tested rather than something specific to the language in which the material was presented.

The fairly heavily factual and scientific emphasis, especially at the upper level of the test, was thought to have been handicapping in one or two countries where the education of students was reported to be primarily literary rather than scientific, and where materials of this sort were described as being quite unfamiliar to them.

All of the suggestions that have been made with respect to the characteristics that entered into item variability must be considered quite tentative. They are all post hoc, and they all depend upon a rather intuitive and judgmental reaction to the items. Certainly, no quantitative statement of the relative importance of linguistic as opposed to cultural factors seems possible. The suggestions made in this section provide at the most very tentative cues for preparing more nearly comparable reading exercises for cross-national comparisons in the future. Even if the suggestions may have some cogency, future workers in this field will not find them particularly easy to apply.

SUMMARY

In this chapter the consistency of item characteristics from country to country has been examined. Reasonably good consistency in difficulty level was found, especially at the lower levels of the test. The consistency was not as high as one had been led to anticipate from some preliminary research, but it does indicate a substantial core of similarity in the Reading Comprehension task as one goes from country to country and from language to language. The consistency in the discrimination indices is somewhat less, but this may well reflect the nature of item selection. Items were selected to give a rather wide spread of difficulties, but as far as possible to give a uniformly high level of discrimination. Thus, chance variations in discrimination would appear larger by comparison. In general, the consistency from country to country was poorer at the higher levels of the test than at the lower. This may reflect greater difficulties in translation, or it may merely reflect greater specialization of the student groups tested in the different countries at the higher levels.

An attempt was made to understand the factors that made for variability in item responses and item difficulty from country to country, but the suggestions that arise from this examination must be considered highly tentative. The differences do appear to stem in part from each of the three main sources that were proposed, to wit, basic differences in the language, problems arising in the specific translation of the text of items, and cultural differences in the general social or educational background of students.

Chapter 10

Relationships Between the Reading Comprehension, Science and Literature Scores

Since the testing in Reading Comprehension took place at the same time as testing in Science and in Literature, and since in most countries the same students took all of the tests that were given in that country, it becomes possible to examine the correlations between achievement in the different subject areas. This is of interest because one views reading as a general educational tool. Hence it is of some concern to know to what extent achievement in the more content oriented subjects is dependent upon reading. It is also of interest to know to what extent achievements in such different subject areas as Science and Literature are related to one another. The Word knowledge test provides an additional measure of the individual's general educational and intellectual background and provides another possible predictor of achievement in the subject areas.

In Tables 10.1, 10.2 and 10.3, correlations are shown for individuals for Populations I, II and IV respectively. In Tables 10.4, 10.5 and 10.6, the corresponding correlations are shown for school averages. A comparison of the correlations for individuals and for school averages is potentially interesting. One can ask whether performance in the school as a unit shows a relatively high degree of consistency across subject areas, or whether schools become specialized, achieving in one subject at the expense of another. An examination of the data on school averages in different countries provides some indication of the degree of specialization within a school and is descriptive of one facet of a country's educational system. This comparison is perhaps particularly of interest in Population IV, where one is dealing with students at the end of their secondary education, and where the probabilities of specialization are somewhat greater.

Let us turn our attention first to relationships for single students. The data for Population I are shown in Table 10.1. Since no Literature test was used at this early level, the correlations involve the

Table 10.1. *Correlations Between Science, Reading Comprehension, Reading Speed and Word Knowledge Scores of Individual Students. Population I*

Country	Science vs. Reading Comprehension	Science vs. Reading Speed	Science vs. Word Knowledge	Reading Comprehension vs. Reading Speed	Reading Comprehension vs. Word Knowledge	Reading Speed vs. Word Knowledge
Belgium (Fl)	.66	.29	.50	.36	.54	.32
Belgium (Fr)	.66	.32	.57	.32	.59	.16
Chile	.62	.25	.46	.29	.54	.29
England	.77	.37	.70	.47	.74	.42
Finland	.71	.32	.58	.36	.62	.27
Hungary	.63	.26	.50	.33	.59	.24
India	.64	.15	.62	.14	.57	.15
Iran	.60	−.03	.46	−.03	.50	−.11
Israel	—	—	—	.32	.65	.25
Italy	.68	.10	.53	.08	.58	.06
Netherlands	.70	.24	.59	.33	.62	.26
Scotland	.75	.39	.70	.48	.72	.44
Sweden	.72	.32	.55	.37	.56	.29
United States	.77	.27	.71	.31	.74	.34
Median	.68	.27	.57	.33	.59	.27

Reading Comprehension, Reading speed and Word knowledge tests on the one hand, and the measure of Science achievement on the other. The most substantial correlation is that between Science and Reading Comprehension. The median correlation is 0.68. This can be compared with a correlation of 0.57 for Word knowledge, and the correlation of Reading Comprehension and Word knowledge of 0.59. All of the correlations involving Reading speed are substantially lower.

It is of some interest to ask how much the three reading tests in combination would predict Science achievement, and how the three should optimally be combined in order to get the highest possible prediction of Science achievement. This analysis has been carried out only for the median of the set of countries, though it could be carried out for each of the countries taken individually. The result shows a multiple correlation of 0.70, indicating that there is relatively little improvement in prediction possible beyond that provided by the Reading Comprehension test alone. The regression weights are as follows: Reading Comprehension 0.52, Word knowledge 0.25, Reading speed 0.03. Thus, it can be seen that the great bulk of the prediction of achievement in Science is provided by the Reading Comprehension test, with the Word knowledge test being a rather poor second and making a little contribution. The measure of speed of reading seems to add essentially no new predictive power as far as improving the estimate of achievement in Science.

A similar analysis can be made for the results from Population II, but here the situation is somewhat complicated by the addition of the Literature measure. One particularly interesting analysis is to inquire what relationship there is between the two content areas for individuals at the same level of general reading ability. That is, what is the correlation between Literature and Science when reading ability is held constant? Since the correlation between the Literature and the Reading Comprehension score is quite high, coming really quite close to the limit set by the reliabilities of the two tests, it would be natural to expect that the partial correlation would be very limited. However, it does seem clear that the Reading Comprehension test is measuring a function somewhat different from the Literature test, because the Reading Comprehension test correlates substantially higher with Science than does the Literature test. The correlations are 0.60 and 0.41 respectively. When Reading Comprehension is held constant, the correlation between Literature and Science (*based on the median of the countries for which data were available*) drops almost exactly to zero. Thus, whatever there is in common between two such different content subjects as Science and Literature, as these abilities are measured in the present enterprise, is provided by the general level of literacy and comprehension of connected prose that is represented by the Reading Comprehension test (see Table 10.2).

Once again it is of interest to consider the whole set of tests as predictors, with first Science and then Literature as the dependent variable to be predicted. These analyses have been carried out and the weights and multiple correlations are shown in a brief tabular format below.

	Science	Literature
Reading Comprehension	0.52	0.58
Word knowledge	0.16	0.14
Reading speed	−0.01	0.06
Other content subject	−0.02	−0.02
Multiple R	0.61	0.69

Table 10.2. *Correlations Between Science, Literature, Reading Comprehension, Reading Speed and Word Knowledge Scores of Individual Students. Population II*

Country	Science vs. Literature	Science vs. Reading Comprehension	Science vs. Reading Speed	Science vs. Word Knowledge	Literature vs. Comprehension	Literature vs. Reading Speed	Literature vs. Word Knowledge	Reading Comprehension vs. Reading Speed	Reading Comprehension vs. Word Knowledge	Reading Speed vs. Word Knowledge
Belgium (Fl)	.34	.53	.23	.43	.66	.27	.51	.31	.59	.28
Belgium (Fr)	.22	.40	−.04	.35	.64	.24	.50	.25	.62	.22
Chile	.41	.54	.14	.34	.62	.21	.46	.28	.51	.24
England	.60	.73	.34	.63	.77	.47	.62	.47	.70	.42
Finland	.41	.60	.25	.48	.69	.44	.55	.47	.65	.43
Hungary	—	.63	.24	.43	—	—	—	.38	.53	.31
India	—	.50	.14	.46	—	—	.34	.07	.39	.08
Iran	.28	.35	.08	.29	.47	.13	—	.14	.43	.13
Israel	—	—	—	—	—	—	—	.40	.67	.36
Italy	.33	.51	.20	.39	.60	.23	.47	.28	.59	.32
Netherlands	—	.60	.13	.49	—	—	—	.28	.62	.25
New Zealand	.52	.70	.33	.59	.75	.50	.59	.50	.68	.48
Scotland	—	.73	.36	.63	—	—	—	.50	.72	.47
Sweden	.48	.65	.23	.50	.72	.36	.51	.40	.60	.30
United States	—	—	—	.60	.74	.52	.58	.55	.69	.46
Median	.41	.60	.23	.47	.68	.32	.51	.38	.62	.31

Table 10.3. *Correlations Between Science, Literature, Reading Comprehension and Word Knowledge Scores of Individual Students. Population IV*

Country	Science vs. Literature	Science vs. Reading Comprehension	Science vs. Word Knowledge	Literature vs. Reading Comprehension	Literature vs. Word Knowledge	Reading Comprehension vs. Word Knowledge
Belgium (Fl)	.24	.50	.33	.59	.45	.50
Belgium (Fr)	.30	.44	.32	.55	.38	.48
Chile	.36	.48	.38	.54	.44	.58
England	.10	.38	.19	.52	.32	.50
Finland	.20	.44	.38	.46	.27	.40
Hungary	—	.53	.34	—	—	.39
India	—	.27	.33	—	—	.32
Iran	.36	.37	.23	.37	.24	.29
Israel	—	—	—	—	—	.51
Italy	.30	.41	.28	.57	.39	.45
Netherlands	—	.28	.21	—	—	.31
New Zealand	.15	.37	.17	.53	.44	.54
Scotland	—	.46	.28	—	—	.58
Sweden	.28	.53	.43	.56	.42	.58
United States	—	—	.54	.69	.51	.68
Median	.28	.44	.32	.54	.38	.50

The results indicate again quite clearly that the prediction of either Literature or Science is mediated almost entirely by the Reading Comprehension test, and that only a small additional prediction is made possible by the addition of Word knowledge, Reading speed, or the other subject matter area. Thus, at this level, there is rather strong evidence that the individual's level of comprehension of connected prose is the common denominator that establishes his level of performance on tests in the two subject areas considered.

In Table 10.3 the analysis has been repeated for the students at the end of secondary school. At this level, all of the correlations are substantially lower. This is a very familiar phenomenon that has occurred repeatedly in these analyses, and that has been identified as resulting from the reduced variability in an end of secondary group in most of the countries with which this study deals. In particular, the correlations between Science and Literature are quite low, and in England and New Zealand they do not differ greatly from zero.

Once again, the regression analysis has been carried out predicting Science from the other variables and predicting Literature from the other variables. No Reading speed test was given at Population IV, so the prediction is from Reading Comprehension, Word knowledge, and the other subject matter area. Although the correlations are substantially smaller, the general pattern is not changed in that most of the predictability is provided by the reading test, a little additional amount is accounted for by the word knowledge measure, and essentially none by the other subject matter score. The weights and multiple correlations appear in the following little tabulation.

	Science	Literature
Reading Comprehension	0.36	0.46
Word knowledge	0.12	0.14
Other content subject	0.04	0.03
Multiple R	0.46	0.56

One can see in each case a rather small increase in the total prediction from adding the other two variables—from 0.44 to 0.46 for Science, and from 0.54 to 0.56 for Literature.

The data for the school averages are shown in Tables 10.4, 10.5 and 10.6. First considering the 10-year-old population, one sees (Table 10.4) that the correlation among class averages is higher in every instance than the correlation for individuals. This is a natural result of the greater stability of class averages and the minimizing of chance errors of measurement in the resulting average score. The effect is most marked in the tests of Science, Reading Comprehension and Word knowledge, which are essentially power tests. Relatively small changes take place as far as the Reading speed test is concerned, and this may very well reflect the fact that accurate timing of this test is an important determiner of score. Since the timing would be uniform within a school, and might vary from school to school, most of the random error resulting from variations in timing would operate across schools and would hold down the correlation between a speed variable and other measures for school averages. The increase in correlation is very general across countries, and for the Reading test versus Science and for the Word knowledge test versus Science there is in each case only one instance in which the correlation over individuals is higher than the correlation of school averages. Thus, differences in schools with respect to their performance in the content subject of Science seem to be rather con-

Country	Science vs. Reading Comprehension	Science vs. Reading Speed	Science vs. Word Knowledge	Reading Comprehension vs. Reading Speed	Reading Comprehension vs. Word Knowledge	Reading Speed vs. Word Knowledge
Chile	.70	.30	.52	.35	.70	.44
England	.88	.43	.87	.45	.88	.42
Finland	.67	.31	.67	.22	.72	.36
Hungary	.66	.39	.42	.40	.70	.38
India	.71	.21	.80	.15	.73	.26
Iran	.76	.16	.62	.06	.77	.05
Israel	—	—	—	.34	.83	.34
Italy	.81	.17	.72	.11	.77	.14
Netherlands	.90	.23	.77	.29	.75	.25
Scotland	.86	.45	.81	.49	.84	.49
Sweden	.85	.32	.72	.40	.75	.37
United States	.91	.52	.90	.48	.92	.53
Median	.81	.31	.72	.34	.76	.36

sistently related to the type of ability represented in the students as shown by the Reading Comprehension test. There is no clear evidence that certain schools do exceptionally well in Science in spite of doing relatively poorly in Reading Comprehension, or vice versa.

At the level of Population II, the 14-year-olds the situation remains much the same (see Table 10.5). Almost universally, the correlations for school averages are higher than the correlations for individuals. This is true both for the correlation of Science with Reading Comprehension, Science with Literature, and Literature with Reading Comprehension. There is at this level almost no indication of specialization of subject matter competence in the sense that certain schools do particularly well in Literature while others do particularly well in Science. The impression conveyed is that within a school the educational system tends to be fairly uniform in its effectiveness and in the progress that it produces in individuals in different subject areas. This progress also seems in each instance to be quite closely related to the general characteristics of the students

Table 10.5. *Between-School Correlations of Science, Literature, Reading Comprehension, Reading Speed and Word Knowledge Tests. Population II*

Country	Science vs. Literature	Science vs. Reading Comprehension	Science vs. Reading Speed	Science vs. Word Knowledge	Literature vs. Reading Comprehension	Literature vs. Reading Speed	Literature vs. Word Knowledge	Reading Comprehension vs. Reading Speed	Reading Comprehension vs. Word Knowledge	Reading Speed vs. Word Knowledge
Chile	.57	.63	.12	.58	.67	.21	.49	.24	.65	.37
England	.80	.90	.53	.88	.92	.66	.88	.59	.92	.53
Finland	.79	.87	.63	.81	.94	.74	.90	.74	.90	.81
Hungary	—	.69	.30	.57	—	—	—	.48	.79	.49
India	—	.61	.26	.62	—	—	—	.24	.60	.22
Israel	.46	—	—	—	—	—	—	.45	.88	.44
Italy	.46	.61	.40	.60	.84	.35	.74	.45	.84	.54
Netherlands	—	.80	.17	.70	—	—	—	.30	.88	.41
New Zealand	.46	.76	.20	.65	.78	.45	.75	.45	.87	.49
Scotland	—	.94	.63	.89	—	—	—	.68	.94	.71
Sweden	.52	.70	.22	.57	.65	.09	.50	.24	.62	.34
United States	.71	.79	.60	.84	.88	.62	.83	.70	.91	.73
Median	.57	.76	.30	.65	.84	.45	.75	.45	.88	.49

Table 10.6. *Between-School Correlations of Science, Literature, Reading Comprehension and Word Knowledge Tests. Population IV*

Country	Science vs. Literature	Science vs. Reading Comprehension	Science vs. Word Knowledge	Literature vs. Reading Comprehension	Literature vs. Word Knowledge	Reading Comprehension vs. Word Knowledge
Belgium (Fr)	.34	.44	.41	.80	.62	.65
Chile	.47	.74	.68	.73	.59	.75
England	−.29	.16	.05	.72	.38	.52
Finland	.20	.42	.56	.50	.39	.40
Hungary	—	.75	.66	—	—	.71
India	—	.38	.62	—	—	.55
Iran	.51	.41	.24	.67	.38	.34
Israel	—	—	—	—	—	.68
Italy	.35	.50	.42	.82	.65	.72
Netherlands	—	.22	.25	—	—	.52
New Zealand	−.19	.20	−.10	.65	.60	.49
Scotland	—	.67	.42	—	—	.66
Sweden	.28	.62	.58	.75	.59	.83
United States	.34	.58	.70	.72	.53	.80
Median	.34	.44	.42	.72	.59	.66

in terms of their ability on a test of reading and/or a test of word knowledge.

Once again, the bulk of the prediction of average achievement in Science or in Literature that is possible for a school is provided by the Reading Comprehension test, and little or no further information is afforded by the other tests that makes it possible to estimate more accurately the average achievement in Science or Literature of the students in the school. The tendency that appeared for individuals for the other subject matter to receive a small negative regression weight is accentuated a little in the school averages correlational analysis, and provides a slight suggestion of specialization in one or the other subject matter. However, regression weights become quite unstable when several predictor variables are as highly intercorrelated as the word knowledge, reading and other subject averages are in these data dealing with school averages. Though there is a trace of evidence of a compensatory effect of Science versus Literature, when Reading Comprehension is held constant, the cues are rather limited and unstable in the light of the size of the correlations referred to above.

Turning now to Population IV, the end of secondary school, one gets a somewhat different picture, at least in certain countries (see Table 10.6). The median correlation between Science and Reading Comprehension is no greater between schools than it is within schools, being 0.44 in both instances. There are four countries in which the correlation is definitely lower between schools than it is within schools. If one looks at the correlation of average Science score versus average Literature score, one finds two countries in which the correlation is just the same between and within schools and two in which it is very dramatically lower. The countries in which the correlation is dramatically lower between schools are England and New Zealand, where the correlations are appreciably negative. That is, the school that excels in Science does poorly in Literature and vice versa. Thus, there is evidence for a sharp specialization of learning at the end of secondary school in England and New Zealand, and a suggestion of a fair amount of specialization in Sweden and Finland. The difference between these countries and the median or typical country comes out most sharply when one looks at the regression weights for predicting achievement in one of the subject matter areas. For example, the regression weights for predicting school average Science achievement based upon the median of countries are: Reading Comprehension 0.30, Word knowledge 0.23, and Literature −0.01. This pattern is not noticeably different from the pattern observed at the lower academic levels. However, if one takes the case of England as perhaps the most dramatic of all, the regression weights appear as follows: Reading Comprehension 0.79, Word knowledge 0.04, and Literature −0.84. These regression weights provide a multiple correlation of 0.61 for predicting Science achievement in a school in England, and this multiple correlation contrasts sharply with the zero order correlations of 0.16 for Reading Comprehension and −0.29 for Literature. In this instance, the compensatory effect comes out most dramatically. It is clear that the achievement of a school in Science is as predictable in England as it is anywhere else, but that it is important to know not merely the students' ability on a general Reading Comprehension test but also their performance on the test in the competing subject of Literature. Given these two items of information, one can make a quite effective prediction of how well the school can do in Science, but the prediction is poor from either one of them taken singly.

174

There has been a good deal of discussion in English educational thinking, especially in the writings of C. P. Snow, of the "Two Culture" phenomenon, as far as education is concerned. The conception is that educated persons are educated in the sciences *or* the humanities, but not both, and that the two groups can scarcely communicate with one another. The results available here for England provide a fairly dramatic documentation of the reality of this phenomenon, but the results over countries indicate that the phenomenon tends to be specific to certain countries, in the present case notably England and New Zealand. A similar calculation of the regression weights for any given country would permit a statement of the degree to which specialization exists and education tends to focus on one versus another field of knowledge. The information on basic skills of reading comprehension and word knowledge enable us to monitor and allow for the general level of ability of the individuals entering the school in question. Thus, in Sweden, where the correlation between schools for Science versus Literature is just the same as it is between individuals, the regression weights come out to be: Reading Comprehension 0.75, Word knowledge 0.20, and Literature -0.40. The multiple correlation is 0.69, compared with a simple correlation of 0.62 for Reading Comprehension taken singly. In contrast, in the United States the weights come out to be Reading Comprehension 0.27, Word knowledge 0.58, Literature -0.10. The simple correlation of 0.70 with Word knowledge, which is the best single predictor for this country, is raised only to 0.73 and very little of the increase is attributable to the inclusion of the Literature score. Here one sees that the achievement in the specific subject matter area is relatively independent of achievement in the other and dependent primarily on the quality of the input as evidenced by the Reading Comprehension and Word knowledge scores. The implication is that United States schools are generally unspecialized, and that performance within a school is consistent across subjects, reflecting the more general ability of the students.

SUMMARY

The brief analyses in this chapter have documented the central role of reading as a determiner of achievement in the more specific subject matter skills. It has been seen that at the elementary and early secondary levels such prediction as can be made of achievement in content subjects comes almost entirely from knowledge of achievement in reading. This is true both of individuals and schools, and the relationship between achievement in subject matter areas is about what would be expected in terms of their dependence upon the common reading ability level of the pupils. By contrast, at the end of secondary school in certain countries there is evidence of marked specialization, and the analysis provides a type of quantitative documentation of the degree to which the specialization does in fact operate.

REFERENCE

Snow, C. P. See, for example, *The Two Cultures: And A Second Look.* Cambridge, England: Cambridge University Press, 1959.

Chapter 11

General Summary and Evaluaiotn

This chapter is devoted to pulling together some of the main findings of the study. These are then examined in an attempt to give some overall picture of what the findings might mean as far as the determinants and correlates of reading achievement are concerned.

Perhaps the most dramatic finding is the very large difference in reading level between the developed and developing countries. Within the group of developed countries the differences are fairly modest, and the rank order shifts from one age group to another. However, with complete consistency the three developing countries fall far below those that have a relatively high level of economic development and a long-standing tradition of universal education. The differences are so large that by the standards of the developed countries, 14-year-olds in the developing countries seem almost illiterate.

A second main finding is that in the developed countries an appreciable prediction of the reading achievement of individual students—and an even more substantial prediction of the average reading achievement of children in a school—is provided by information about their home and family backgrounds. A dominant determiner of the outcome from a school in terms of reading performance is the input in terms of the kinds of students that go to the school. When the population of a school comes from homes in which the parents are themselves well educated, economically advantaged, and able to provide an environment in which reading materials and communications media are available, the school shows a generally superior level of reading achievement.

These two findings are basically consistent with one another, because the developed countries differ from the developing ones perhaps most sharply in just those characteristics that characterize the children in the developed countries who read well. That is, the developed countries are in general able to provide an environment in which the parents are educated, in which books and magazines are available, and in which the media of radio and television are accessible to all the children. It is, then, not surprising that the children in these countries are better readers than those from the countries in which these amenities are the exception rather than the rule.

As one turns to the information about schools and schooling, the results are somewhat disheartening as far as providing cues as to what aspects of a school organization or program contribute to the reading ability of the children in the school. In general, the factors that it was possible to identify in the school are at best minimally related to reading achievement, and a relationship that is found in any country rarely appears consistently in the others. Even the variables that one might anticipate a priori would be predictors of achievement do not tend to hold up. For example, indicators of training of teachers in the teaching of reading, of size of class, and of availability of specialist teachers in the school all turn out to have either no relationship to reading achievement or a relationship the reverse of what one might anticipate. Thus, the presence of remedial teachers in a school and efforts to individualize teaching by grouping within a class or giving individual instruction to students have, if anything, a negative relationship to measured reading ability.

One must, indeed, be extremely cautious in interpreting results such as these, because one does not know which way any causation flows or whether the relationship is an incidental reflection of some quite different underlying factor. Thus, it is entirely possible that where a negative relationship appears between some measure of individualization and reading achievement, this may mean that in those schools in which teachers are faced with a large number of poor readers, teachers make special provisions in an attempt to deal with those problems. Then adaptations become a result, rather than a cause of the reading difficulties. By the same token, the failure to find any relationship between class size and achievement may mean that small classes are found in isolated rural areas, or that children who are having difficulty are put in small classes so that more specialized attention may be given to them. Although one is very hesitant to attach any meaning to some of the relationships that appear, in total it must be admitted that the study provides very little evidence of the impact of the school or of specific school factors on the progress of students in reading.

This finding is perhaps not too surprising. It certainly does not imply that schooling "does not make a difference". It may merely imply that the schools that have been studied all represent at least a basic level of competence, and that beyond that the differences between scools are either inadequately assessed by our instruments or are of minor importance as far as achievement is concerned. After all, the home is the primary and continuing source of influence on a child, and the school has impact on him for a relatively small number of hours a day and often for only half the days in the year. Thus, it is perhaps unrealistic to expect to find in the types of indicators of school characteristics that we were able to assemble by questionnaire media from administrators, teachers and students very much that has a demonstrable effect on the achievement of the child.

In final summary, then, the clear result is that good home and environmental backgrounds provide strong differentiation between countries and, within countries, between students.